Paddle your own Canoe

Paddle your own Canoe

Gary & Joanie McGuffin

A BOSTON MILLS PRESS BOOK

First published in 1999 by
BOSTON MILLS PRESS
132 Main Street, Erin, Ontario, Canada N0B 1T0
Tel: (519) 833-2407   Fax: (519) 833-2195
e-mail: books@boston-mills.on.ca   www.boston-mills.on.ca

An affiliate of
STODDART PUBLISHING CO. LIMITED
34 Lesmill Road, Toronto, Ontario, Canada M3B 2T6
Tel: (416) 445-3333   Fax: (416) 445-5967
e-mail: gdsinc@genpub.com   www.genpub.com

Distributed in Canada by
General Distribution Services Inc.
325 Humber College Boulevard, Toronto, Ontario, Canada M9W 7C3
Orders (Ontario & Quebec): 1-800-387-0141
Orders (NW Ontario & other provinces): 1-800-387-0172
e-mail: customerservice@ccmailgw.genpub.com
Canadian TELEBOOK: S1150391

Distributed in the United States by
General Distribution Services Inc.
85 River Rock Drive, Suite 202, Buffalo, New York 14207-2170
Toll-free: 1-800-805-1083   Toll-free fax: 1-800-481-6207
e-mail: gdsinc@genpub.com
www.genpub.com
PUBNET: 6307949

03 02 01 00 99   1 2 3 4 5

CATALOGING IN PUBLICATION DATA

McGuffin, Gary

Paddle your own canoe

ISBN 1-55046-214-8

1. Canoes and canoeing.
I. McGuffin, Joanie.   II. Title.
GV783.M383 1999   797.1' 22   C98-931657-2

Copyright © Gary and Joanie McGuffin 1999

Photography by Gary McGuffin and Hugh Trueman

Book design by Hugh Trueman, Registered Graphic Designer, 45 Degrees Corporation

Film work by Rainbow Digicolor Inc., Toronto

Printed in Canada by Friesen Printers

OVERLEAF: (left) The Gull River, Ontario; (right) Gord Lake, in the ancient forest headwaters of the Algoma Highlands.
OPPOSITE: Camping near Pic Island on the north shore of Lake Superior.

We acknowledge for their financial support of our publishing program the Government of Canada through the Book Publishing Industry Development Program (BPIDP), the Canada Council, and the Ontario Arts Council.

To the canoe,
for all the places it takes us and all the joy it brings.

Contents

The golden mist of dawn casts a magical spell over Megisan Lake, assuring us of a good day's paddling ahead.

1 The Way of the Canoe

For us, canoeing is much more than a physical pursuit; it is a way of life. When Gary and I load our packs into the canoe, whether for a few days or a few months, we feel a renewed sense of freedom. We enjoy living by a different calendar and clock. Time is measured in sunrises and sunsets and seasonal patterns. When the warm east winds arrive to break up the ice on our bay, we shovel away the last of the snow piled against the barn door. The canoes are inside where we left them last November, at rest on their racks, waiting. They are our wild horses and the very sight of them stirs our souls. Soon another adventure will begin.

Sometimes we chose a river run riding the high waters of spring melt. Other years, we push off from Lake Superior's shore when the north-facing slopes are still snow covered and shaded rock cuts are laden with gigantic icicles. With the returning light and warmth come the birds: sandhill cranes, blue herons, loons, sandpipers, hawks, eagles, warblers, and a host of other songbirds. Tiny forest flowers blooming along greening portage trails, a cow moose with her twin calves, a black bear with her cubs, and the rush of water everywhere — all are welcome signs of new life.

As far back as we can both remember, we have lived with canoes. For me, it was the 16-foot red cedar canvas canoe that my parents bought the year they built a summer cottage in the Muskoka lakes. When I was four years old, those lakes seemed like oceans and the shoreline miles endless. We had our secret destinations, places we could get to only by canoe: swimming holes, cliffs and caves at the water's edge, a haunted house in the ragged undergrowth of a small island, and portage paths to ponds where the beavers built their lodges and dams. Perhaps my most vivid memories are those of nighttime drifting trips, where we floated for hours beneath open skies on black waters reflecting the Milky Way, shooting stars, and the northern lights.

Long before Gary and I knew one another, canoes were part of our lives, from summer's idyllic exploring to winter's readings of the classics. We read Holling C. Holling's *Paddle-to-the-Sea*, Farley Mowat's *Lost in the Barrens*, Grey Owl's *Men of the Last Frontier,* and many other stories that took place on real lakes and rivers that we could find in atlases at home and school. We dreamed of leading an adventurous life traveling by canoes through wild places.

We both grew up on the fringe of cities that had waterways running through them. Medway Creek and the Thames River were a short hike from Gary's home in London. My home in Thornhill on the edge of Toronto had the Credit, the Humber, and the Don Rivers. These rivers reminded us that cities were built upon nature. The valleys of these rivers were our wild space for part of the year until we each migrated

One of North America's greatest systems of canoe routes, summer portages, and winter trails lies in Northern Ontario's Temagami region. For more than 6,000 years, people have traveled the nastawgan, stopping to admire nature's landmarks. This is Centre Falls on the Lady Evelyn River.

north with our families for the summer. Here our canoeing experiences differed.

Muskoka was my summer hideaway, a picturesque cottage country where everyone seemed to have a canoe lying on the dock, whether they paddled often or not. Canoes were simply part of summer and part of cottage tradition. They meant daytrips, island picnics, and slipping quietly in and out of bays watching for mink and beaver.

Gary's family traveled north to a place called Temagami, meaning "deep water." The canoe was as much a part of this place as Temagami was part of the canoe. Nowhere in all of North America had the glaciers scribed such an intricate tracery of lakes and rivers. The aboriginal people who still live here have ancestral links spanning two hundred generations. Little wonder that a vast network of water and land routes evolved here. Known as *nastawgan*, these routes were everywhere marked by blazes old and new, portage trails, traditional campsites, pictograph walls, trappers' cabins.

When Gary was four, he met Mr. McLean, an old prospector whose cabin was near the family camp. He took Gary for his first canoe ride in his hand-built cedar canvas canoe. When Gary's parents built a summer camp in a more remote part of the lake, they granted him use of the canoe whenever he wished as long as he wore his lifejacket. So together with his dog, Rusty, Gary spent many an idyllic summer exploring bays by canoe, beach-combing, and following animal trails. They would lie in the bottom of the canoe together watching the shifting clouds. Sometimes they drifted off to sleep until Rusty would awaken, ears pricked at the sound of tree branches scratching the hull, nose quivering with the smells of the forest. To Gary, the canoe was like a bicycle is to a child in the city. Freedom.

For our first journey together, we paddled a canoe to James Bay. It was autumn on the Missinaibi River, traveling alone, just the two of us camping in the wildest places I had ever known. Some days were warm, and we paddled the rapids and drifted with the current catching fish to eat with our bannock bread twice a day. Some days we bowed our heads against the early snows. Great flocks of Canada and snow geese caught these southbound winds. By the time we reached salt water, we had planned our next adventure, a 2,100-mile (3,400 km) backpacking trip through the Appalachian mountains following a marked footpath from Georgia to Maine. On exactly the same date one year later, the big walk was complete. We stood upon the summit of the final peak, Mount Katahdin in Maine, looking east to the Atlantic and north to Canada. Our journey into the future together seemed to be taking shape along with ripening plans to paddle across Canada.

Eighteen months later, young and married, we launched our canoe into the Gulf of St. Lawrence to begin a two-season, 6,000-mile (10,000 km) paddle to the Arctic Ocean. It never really occurred to us how much a journey of this kind represented the physical unity of a nation, its aboriginal and European history, its people, landscape, waterways, and its spirit. What we learned on this first voyage was the power of a journey by canoe. It was a personal endeavor, yet as our stories were transmitted weekly by radio and newspaper across the country, our journey became part of other people's lives, too.

Beneath the tame veneer of civilization, there is a wildness that lurks in all of us. It is the spirit of adventure. Step into a canoe, pick up a paddle, and you become one with the wind and water. Learning to canoe is a journey both inward and outward, and it can easily be a lifelong pursuit. Our parents gave us the gift of their encouragement in our canoeing life. We now pass this gift along to you in the writing of this book.

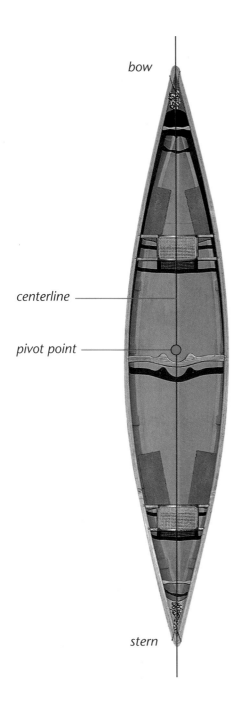

bow

centerline

pivot point

stern

2 The Outfit

About Canoes

Pick up a canoe catalog today and you'll get a quick education in the many different kinds of canoes available. Technological improvements encouraged in the competitive field have spilled over into the recreational field, spawning a wide range of highly specialized canoes that are suited to any individual's requirements. The choice is almost overwhelming. Yet these choices are only embellishments to a form that has been around for a long time.

Paddling a birchbark canoe for the first time, I was impressed by how lively and responsive it was and how strong it felt, not fragile at all. The bark as thick as leather, the familiar white paper turned in, and the inside of the hull covered with cedar planking and ribs — this was not a museum artifact, it was a very real example of a craft used for thousands of years. One paddle stroke and it swirled upon the water with the lightness of a pirouetting dancer, a crisp leaf caught by a breeze. Two strokes forward and it was as if I were skimming over ice.

A Canoeist's Vocabulary

Chine: the curve of the canoe where the sides meet the bottom. The sharpness of this curve influences secondary stability when the canoe is tipped to one side or the other. Flat-bottomed canoes with vertical sides have abrupt or hard chines. They are stable when at rest on calm water, but when the canoe is tipped to one side they are unstable. Depending on other aspects of the canoe's design, this instability can increase the canoe's responsiveness to turning. But when the canoe is edged (tipped) the wrong way, hard chines are less forgiving than soft chines.

Flare: the progressive widening of the hull from the waterline to the gunwales, which serves to deflect water and increase stability.

Freeboard: the distance from the waterline to the top edge of the gunwale. Increased load settles the canoe into the water, therefore decreasing the freeboard.

Keel line: a line running from bow to stern along the centerline on the underside of the hull.

Sheer: the longitudinal profile from amidships to the ends of the canoe along the top edge of the gunwales.

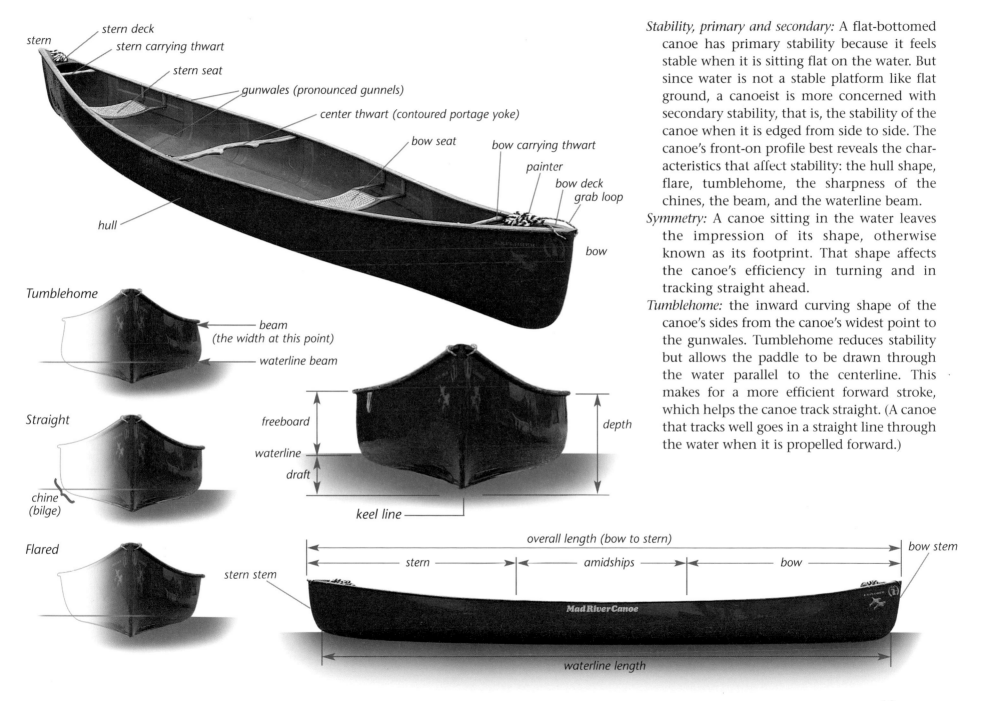

stern
stern deck
stern carrying thwart
stern seat
gunwales (pronounced gunnels)
center thwart (contoured portage yoke)
bow seat
bow carrying thwart
painter
bow deck
grab loop
hull
bow

Tumblehome

beam
(the width at this point)
waterline beam

Straight

chine
(bilge)

freeboard
waterline
draft

depth

keel line

Flared

stern stem

overall length (bow to stern)
stern
amidships
bow
bow stem

Mad River Canoe

waterline length

Stability, primary and secondary: A flat-bottomed canoe has primary stability because it feels stable when it is sitting flat on the water. But since water is not a stable platform like flat ground, a canoeist is more concerned with secondary stability, that is, the stability of the canoe when it is edged from side to side. The canoe's front-on profile best reveals the characteristics that affect stability: the hull shape, flare, tumblehome, the sharpness of the chines, the beam, and the waterline beam.

Symmetry: A canoe sitting in the water leaves the impression of its shape, otherwise known as its footprint. That shape affects the canoe's efficiency in turning and in tracking straight ahead.

Tumblehome: the inward curving shape of the canoe's sides from the canoe's widest point to the gunwales. Tumblehome reduces stability but allows the paddle to be drawn through the water parallel to the centerline. This makes for a more efficient forward stroke, which helps the canoe track straight. (A canoe that tracks well goes in a straight line through the water when it is propelled forward.)

13

A Comparison of Canoe Shapes

We paddle more than one design of canoe. Each canoe has its own set of characteristics that make it more suitable for one type of paddling than for another. For instance, the solo flatwater canoe shown here has a fairly straight keel line. This means it is good for straight-ahead paddling, as in lake-to-lake canoeing. We describe this feature of a canoe as having good *tracking ability,* because it goes more naturally in a straight line.

Rocker is the degree of curve in the canoe's hull from bow to stern along the keel line. The more rocker in the hull, the more the bow and stern ends are raised and kept from making contact with the water. In this way the ends provide less resistance to turning.

The tandem whitewater canoe has full ends with lots of flare, which deflects waves, making it very seaworthy. Paddlers remain drier longer in rough conditions in this kind of "dry canoe." The canoe we use for flatwater tandem paddling is an all-purpose canoe good for lake-to-lake traveling, easy whitewater, and for carrying a week's supply of canoe-tripping gear.

Looking at the variations in this wondrous form, you can see why some canoes are faster and are better able to hold a straight course than others, and some are better able to spin and turn. A canoe's waterline length and beam, the degree of rocker, and the symmetry of the hull all affect maneuverability, speed, stability, and cargo capacity. These considerations must be weighed one against the other. If you enjoy many different kinds of canoeing as we do, then it seems there is no such thing as the one perfect canoe.

At right are four of the canoes we used in the making of this book. Shown here in three perspectives, they illustrate the ways different design features affect a canoe's performance.

1   This fast, lightweight canoe was used to demonstrate many of the solo flatwater maneuvers in this book. The streamlined, shallow V-shaped hull has a relatively straight keel line that emphasizes forward speed and excellent tracking ability. This canoe has flare above the waterline in the bow and stern to shed waves and keep the canoe dry, but it also has tumblehome at the center to make it easier for you to paddle more efficiently. When you hold the canoe on edge (tipped to one side), you can touch the gunwale to the water without capsizing. Edging allows you to turn this graceful craft with relative ease even though its characteristics are better suited to tracking straight. The lightweight Kevlar construction makes it as light as a small child to lift (35 lbs, or 16 kg). This canoe requires minimal paddling effort for lake and river cruising, whether for one day or several days at a time.

2   This tandem canoe is the most general purpose of the four designs shown. We used this particular model for all the tandem flatwater maneuvers demonstrated here. It is a tried and true design predictable in a variety of river and lake conditions, whether you are carrying a load or paddling it empty. It has a relatively straight keel line with a slight rocker, which makes it both easy to track and turn. The 16-foot, 4-inch (5.1 m), symmetrical, shallow-V hull has lots of load-carrying capacity. It has plenty of freeboard for two people, comfortably carrying enough food and supplies for a two-week canoe trip. This particular canoe, which is also constructed of lightweight Kevlar, weighs only 54 pounds (24.5 kg).

3   This is one of the two models of solo whitewater canoe that we used for this book. I love this little 12-foot (3.5 m) canoe. The extreme rocker and the more rounded V-shaped hull makes it highly responsive to subtle changes in weight shift. Although less forgiving when you tip the wrong way, there is a tradeoff. This is an excellent design for surfing waves, carving turns, and whitewater playboating. This canoe is easy to roll and to paddle upstream hopping eddy to eddy. The depth and flare make it a dry canoe, and the hull shape definitely favors turning over tracking.

4   This tandem whitewater canoe is suited both for river trips and for just plain fun playing in whitewater. Like the solo whitewater canoe, this model is constructed of a material called Royalex. Although heavier than fiberglass or Kevlar, this is a very durable material. The moderate rocker in this canoe means paddlers can spin it on a dime. The symmetrical, shallow-V'd, 16-foot (5 m) hull of moderate width gives this canoe great secondary stability. It is responsive yet forgiving if you tip the wrong way. There's lots of freeboard even when it is loaded for an extended trip. There are more specialized tandem whitewater canoes that are faster, more responsive, narrower, and extremely rockered, but we like this one for its more general-purpose characteristics necessary for river tripping.

1   Solo Flatwater

2   Tandem Flatwater

 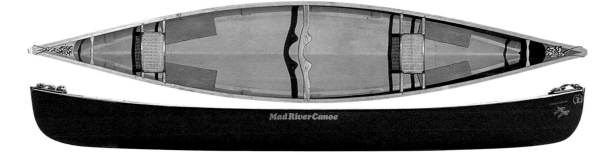

3   Solo Whitewater

4   Tandem Whitewater

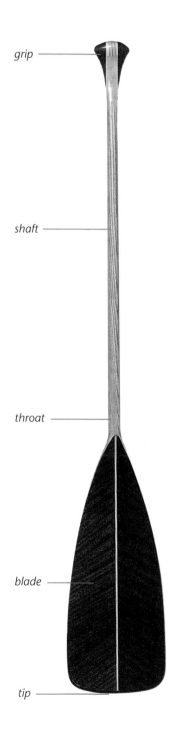

grip

shaft

throat

blade

tip

The Paddle

Paddle selection is a personal affair. Our fondness for paddles made of wood has never wavered. The natural flex and buoyancy of wooden paddles allows them to communicate the feel of the water. The combination of rigidity with slight flex provides good shock absorption for a paddler's joints. Wood is warm on the hands in spring and fall, and it makes a comforting and aesthetically pleasing contrast to all the synthetic materials used in paddlesports today. Everything from canoe hulls to gunwales to seats is constructed from plastics, vinyl, carbon fibers, Kevlar, fiberglass and Royalex. In canoeing, the traditional wood canoe paddle is becoming our last natural link to the wild places we paddle through. These paddles are our traveling companions. We respect and care for them like best friends.

Hanging on our cabin wall are four paddles. These are the ones Gary used from the time he was four until he was sixteen. His first paddle was scaled perfectly to fit a child. It is 42 inches (107 cm) long with a blade 4 inches (10 cm) wide. The 3/4-inch (2 cm) diameter shaft and 2-inch (5 cm) grip were made for small hands. Even young canoeists enjoy paddles that fit. Over the years, Gary painted colorful designs on the blades of his paddles. During the summer before our Missinaibi adventure, I made my first paddle, from ash wood for strength. Sawing, sanding, filing, and finishing revealed the beautiful linear grain. I was proud of my efforts, and it was a hefty bit of workmanship that gave me as good an arm workout as any set of barbells.

Gary especially loves fixing and refinishing paddles. On a cold, stormy night with all the canoes safely stored on their racks in the barn, he'll pick up a paddle. He works slowly and quietly, lightly sanding the shaft and finishing the fine edges of its blade. Memories of lake passages and river runs are rekindled by such handiwork. And a few new dreams are set in motion, too.

We would encourage you to try and make a paddle from wood when you have the time, tools and inclination. In the process, you'll learn a lot about what makes a paddle feel right. But for the time being, we'll provide some advice about paddle types, paddle sizing, and how to hold the paddle properly.

Paddle Types

From grip to blade, the attributes of paddles vary greatly, depending on their intended use, the materials from which they are made, and their construction. We use the six paddles shown in the photo at right for a variety of canoeing experiences.

The whitewater paddle is a strong, straight-shafted paddle constructed from laminations of ash, cherry and basswood. The blade and shaft are wrapped with fiberglass. The T-grip provides your control hand with a strong, solid grasp of the paddle when you are

There are many paddle designs to choose from. Shown here are some of our favorites. From left to right: whitewater, bent-shaft, freestyle, voyageur, beavertail, ottertail.

The Two Faces of the Paddle

Throughout this book, we have distinguished the two sides of the paddle blade to show clearly the *powerface* and the *backface*. The light-colored side is the powerface and the dark-colored side is the backface. It's a good idea, especially when learning, to mark your paddles clearly with colored tape or paint so that you can recognize the two sides immediately. With your own two-colored blade in hand, you can more easily follow the instruction sequences in this book.

How to Size the Paddle

Crouch down to approximate the height that you are from the water when seated in the canoe. Place the paddle grip on the ground and hold the paddle shaft vertical. The throat of the paddle should be close to nose-high. For an even better measure, sit in the canoe on the water. Hold the paddle vertical with your hands on the grip and shaft. Submerge the entire blade up to the throat. The grip should be level with your nose.

The Control Hand and Thumb

The *control hand* holds the paddle grip. The thumb on this hand, the *control thumb,* becomes an important point of reference when you are learning maneuvers. For example, when describing the J-stroke, we'll talk about turning your control thumb forward, which means that your control hand will rotate forward with the control thumb pointing forward.

maneuvering in rough water. In contrast, the pear grip on the bent-shaft and freestyle paddles has a better feel rolling in the palm of your hand when you are traveling or playing on flatwater. These three paddles sport reinforced tips and edges to prevent wear and tear.

The bent-shaft paddle evolved to suit the purposes of long-distance flatwater racing. The angle of the shaft puts the blade in a perpendicular position at the end of the stroke, which means you are not lifting water, making it highly efficient for straight-ahead speed. We have used them on all of our longer journeys. Pick up the heavier whitewater paddle in one hand and the lighter freestyle or marathon paddle in the other and you can feel the compromise made between the attributes of strength and light weight.

The other three paddles, the voyageur, beavertail, and ottertail, are traditional solid-wood designs of varying blade shapes. They are rounded, longer, narrower blades good for general-purpose paddling.

The Shaft Hand and How to Hold the Paddle

Your *shaft hand* holds the paddle shaft. The point at which you hold on to the shaft depends on the type of stroke you are doing. One way to judge the correct spacing of the shaft hand from the control hand is to push the grip of the paddle into your armpit. Extend your arm down the paddle shaft, marking the spot you can reach with the tips of your fingers. This is where the top of your shaft hand grips the shaft. For sizing, as a general rule, there should be about 4 to 6 inches (10–15 cm) of shaft between the bottom of your shaft hand and the blade. Now extend your control hand out in front of you, holding on to the grip. Let the paddle hang down and, reaching out with your shaft hand, grasp the shaft in the correct position, 4 to 6 inches (10–15 cm) up from the blade. Rotate your control thumb forward as you would in the recovery phase of the forward stroke. The shaft rotates *freely* through the shaft hand as if it were an oar in an oarlock. The powerface turns out. If you rotate your control thumb back, the powerface will turn in, revealing the backface of the blade.

Hypothermia, a Canoeist's Greatest Danger

All paddlers should be able to recognize and react to hypothermia. When the core temperature of a human body begins to drop because of cold-water immersion or exposure to cold air and wind, this is hypothermia. It is a life-threatening situation. Far more people die in the water of hypothermia than do of drowning.

Hypothermia begins with shivering as your body tries to warm itself. When the shivering becomes uncontrollable shaking and you start to lose motor skills, you are also losing judgment and reasoning power. Once the body is losing heat faster than making it, physical and mental collapse follows, making it impossible for you to help yourself in any way.

One rainy September day, while on our first canoe trip together, paddling the Missinaibi River to James Bay, I got hypothermia. I was too shy to complain of being wet and cold. Late in the afternoon Gary noticed that I was paddling weakly, and when he asked if everything was okay, I was incoherent. He reacted quickly, paddling us to shore to set up camp. I was physically unable to get myself out of the canoe, make a fire, or change into dry clothes. Without Gary's help, I would have been in serious trouble. Several hot chocolates and two hours later I finally stopped shaking. Your body's reaction to gradually cooling conditions will depend on your personal metabolism. Some people warm up and cool down more quickly than others. Every paddler should have first-aid training and know how to deal with hypothermia.

The best approach to hypothermia is to avoid it in the first place. Dress appropriately and stay dry. For those who think in Fahrenheit, a general rule is to add the air and water temperature together. If the result is less than 100, be prepared for hypothermia. (This is the 100-degree rule; metric thinkers follow the 35-degree rule.)

Dressing for Flatwater

1 *A warm day on the water requires a minimum of clothing. We do, however, don sunscreen, Tilley hat, sunglasses, some kind of protective footwear such as sandals, and a lifejacket (PFD). In many places, carrying and/or wearing a personal flotation device (PFD) is now mandatory. In the event of a capsize, PFDs provide buoyancy and warmth and allow you to save your energy for rescuing yourself and your equipment. The important thing is for your PFD to fit snugly without slipping up to your ears if you go for a swim. Only Coast Guard-approved Type III (vest-type) jackets are suitable and comfortable for canoeing. Wear your PFD in a canoe just as you wear a helmet when on a bicycle: it is there to protect you, and as adults we can set a good example for children by wearing them ourselves.*

2 *A warm day on the water can quickly turn cool if a breeze comes up, the weather changes, or the sun goes down. The clothing shown here, a fleece jacket and windproof outerwear, is terrific for a canoeist because it is quick drying, maintains warmth, and is lightweight and compressible.*

3 *Being prepared for cold and/or wet weather is essential in certain climates, seasons, and on multi-day canoe trips. Not only does getting wet and cold take away from the enjoyment of canoeing, it can be dangerous. Since most of your heat escapes through your head, wear a wool or fleece hat on a cold day. Dress in layers for versatility. We wear silk, wool, or polyester long underwear, a breathable, waterproof parka and pants, a fleece or wool sweater, and pogies. Pogies protect your hands, greatly helping you maintain your dexterity on a cold day. Depending on the conditions, wear lightweight hiking boots or rubber boots.*

Even when planning a short trip on a warm day, it is a good idea to be prepared for the unexpected. This list of daytripping essentials can be added to depending on the weather.

- a waterproof dry bag containing a change of clothes (these can include an extra fleece or wool sweater, a windproof shell, waterproof jacket and pants, a hat)
- sunscreen and sunglasses
- drinking water and a high-energy snack
- basic first-aid kit and the know-how to use it
- pocket knife, duct tape, and pliers for simple repairs
- matches in a waterproof container
- map and flashlight

3 Balancing the Body

If Gary and I approached canoeing as a competitive sport, then our journeys would represent weeks and months of honing skills, developing endurance, and building strength. We admire dedication to perfection in any pursuit; after all, it is within the competitive world that new ideas emerge and, for example, more efficient paddling techniques evolve. Those techniques developed by competitive canoeists can be applied to recreational paddling.

If you have ever watched the lithe, fluid movements of a wolf as compared to those of a domestic dog, you can appreciate the beauty of efficiency in motion. People who paddled canoes long ago probably paddled with the same finesse that athletes of today strive for, because canoeing for them was not a matter of winning, but more a matter of survival.

Canoeing may not be a matter of survival for us, but paddling efficiently has many benefits. Canoeing efficiently is good for your body. It means less stress and strain on joints and small muscles because the effort is spread out over your whole body. *Canoeing efficiently means going farther faster, with less effort.*

All our lives, in every season, we have enjoyed a variety of physical pursuits. We can't help but compare canoeing to telemark skiing, dancing, gymnastics, and skating. In all these activities, your body's balance point is your belly button. Keep your body centered over this point and you will be balanced. *Efficient technique, be it in paddling or otherwise, has far more to do with balancing the body — maintaining your equilibrium*

with control and finesse — than with brute strength.

Years ago we adopted yoga and its fluid pattern of postures, attention to breathing, and mind-freeing exercise as a complement to our canoeing. We have found that by performing a sequence of balanced motions based on the natural movements of the spine, overall flexibility and balance are greatly improved.

Yoga postures are body positions that are performed in sequence, each in a static and dynamic phase. Each posture is held for a short time in a relaxed but attentive manner. While in the motionless phase, pay attention to your stretched muscles and your breathing. The dynamic phase involves moving fluidly from one posture to another. Breathe slowly, deeply, and naturally. Inhale while lifting your legs, arms, and torso, and exhale when lowering them. Yoga fosters a supple, flexible body. Muscles and tendons that are limber are less subject to injury.

By learning to control our breathing we can control our bodies in magic ways. A quiet mind is an open and aware mind. You gain the greatest benefit from yoga in this state.

1 *Sitting posture: Fold your right leg then left leg underneath buttocks with the soles of your feet turned up and heels out. Place hands on thighs, keeping back, neck, and head straight.*

Yoga also helps visualization, an awake dreaming state, in which we see and feel ourselves accomplishing something before we physically do it. Visualize yourself performing maneuvers correctly and getting to where you want to go, and with practice you will be successful.

The Canoeist's Spine

Yoga, like canoeing, can be a lifelong pursuit. One of its great benefits is in maintaining a naturally flexible spine and good posture. The canoeist's kneeling stance that we recommend throughout this book puts the least amount of pressure on your spine while at the same time providing for stability and allowing the greatest range of motion.

2 Lie on your stomach with head turned to one side, legs relaxed, heels splayed outward, and arms resting by sides. Inhale and exhale deeply, feeling the ground beneath you.

3 Full locust: Lying on your stomach, place chin on ground, arms by sides, legs together. Slowly and smoothly raise legs and chest from the ground while inhaling. Hold your breath and the posture, then exhale while lowering legs to the ground.

4 Cobra posture: Lie on your stomach, legs together, palms on the ground with fingertips at shoulders. Tuck elbows in. Raise head slowly, eyes to the sky. Your head, chest, and abdomen are raised, but your belly button stays touching the ground.

5 Full bow: Lie flat on your stomach, legs spread a little, arms at sides with chin on ground. Grasp ankles with hands and slowly raise head from ground, looking skyward. Raise thighs from ground by pressing feet against hands. Hold, then lower smoothly.

6 Half plough consists of three stages that all begin similarly. Lie on your back, legs together, palms on ground. Keep knees straight. Half plough, stage 1 (not shown): Raise and lower one leg at a time, beginning with the right leg. Stage 2 (shown): Raise both legs together in increments of 30, then 60, then 90 degrees.

7 Half plough, stage 2 continued: Raise legs together on an inhalation and lower on an exhalation. Keep chin tucked in so neck and head are pressed to the ground and shoulders are relaxed. Stage 3 (not shown): Raise legs together to the 90-degree position. Press palms and arms against ground, raising buttocks, and lower legs beyond head until they are parallel with the ground.

8 Full plough (shown): From stage 3 of half plough, extend and lower legs until toes touch the ground. Slowly return legs to parallel position, then up to the 90-degree position, and lower to 60 and 30 degrees and back to the ground. Concentrate on your spine, lowering vertebra by vertebra to the ground.

9 Forward bend, stage 1: Stand erect with toes forward, feet together, and weight equally distributed. Knees are relaxed with shoulders back and down. Slowly raise arms straight up to your ears.

10 Forward bend, stage 2: Bend back from the waist, squeezing the buttocks. Then leaning forward from the lower spine, with your back straight, reach out with straight arms and outstretched fingertips. Lead with your chin.

14 Wheel posture: Take a wide stance with feet facing forward. Raise left arm until it is level with your shoulder. Turn palm up, raising arm to ear. Bend upper body from the waist, stretching on left and kinking on right. Repeat on other side.

15 Boat posture: With legs outstretched, arms at sides, and palms on ground, slowly raise legs together. Balance on buttocks, then raise hands, reaching out toward your knees. Breathe rhythmically. Lower legs and straighten back while exhaling.

16 Twist posture: Place your right foot on the outside of left knee. Place right arm with straight elbow behind your back, palm flat and fingers facing back. Reach left arm across bent right leg. Keep arm straight with left elbow pressed against right thigh. Straighten back and twist spine, looking over right shoulder. Repeat on other side.

11 *Forward bend, stage 3: Reach forward until bend is complete. Arms, shoulders, neck, and head hang totally relaxed. Holding legs, gently encourage head to knees at each breath. Straighten, unfurling like a fern.*

12 *Triangle posture, stage 1: Take a wide stance with feet forward. Extend arms sideways in line with your shoulders. Turn left foot 45 degrees, then turn your body to left side and bend from waist, bringing your right hand to your left foot.*

13 *Triangle posture, stage 2: With your left arm stretched up, turn head to look into left palm. Maintain twist, raise your body, then turn forward. Repeat steps on other side.*

17 *Warrior posture, stage 1: Fold legs beneath buttocks. Rest buttocks on insteps. With back, neck, and head straight, bring both arms behind you, grasping the right wrist with the thumb and index finger of the left hand.*

18 *Warrior posture, stage 2: Leading with your chin, bend forward until your forehead touches the ground. Keep your buttocks resting on your insteps, hands still clasped behind you. Let your elbows relax. Return to upright by unfurling your spine.*

19 *Total relaxation: Lie on your back, palms up, legs outstretched, feet splayed outward, and eyes half closed. Visualize each part of your body relaxing bit by bit, working up from the toes. Relax completely — but without falling asleep.*

4 The Fundamentals of Paddling

The Paddler's Box

The paddler's box is an imaginary cube that contains the upper body. By paddling within the paddler's box, you are encouraged to use the muscles of your torso, which have much more strength and endurance than your arm muscles. By keeping your arms within the "box," you can avoid muscle strain and shoulder dislocations.

The Body in Motion

As a gymnast, I learned while doing handsprings that the spring and power did not come from my arms but rather through my shoulders and the larger muscles of my torso. We learned about turning our bodies into coiled springs through rotation. I remember how the instructor had us standing with our arms outstretched, palms flat, 6 inches (15 cm) from the wall. "Touch the wall," she said, "without moving anything but your shoulders. That movement is where the power of your spring is found." Therein lies one of the most important concepts of proper canoeing technique: rotation. In that same movement, the act of turning your shoulder plane to the side, is found the power of your paddle strokes. In order for paddle strokes to be both safe and effective, *your body has to rotate before every stroke.*

Going back to the yoga, you'll remember the importance we placed on improving the natural movements of the spine. With good flexibility, a canoeist's upper body and lower body are able to work independently. As soon as you step into a canoe, you, the paddler, have grown two new appendages — a canoe and a paddle. Think of wearing the canoe instead of just sitting in it. The canoe is an extension of your lower body. The paddle, then, is a specialized extension of your arms and upper body.

This approach is essential for keeping your weight and balance over the canoe's centerline. Your upper body should not lean out over the water and your paddles are not meant to be weight-bearing water wings. Instead, your upper body should remain fairly upright with the lower half adopting the shape of a J by weighting and unweighting your knees. This is called a *J-lean.* For more about the J-lean, see Chapter 7, Getting Centered.

Paddling Principles and Newton's Laws of Motion

As paddlers, it is important to understand that we, as a part of all of Nature, are subject to certain rules that dictate movement. It is also helpful to know that whether you are an expert or novice paddler, your body, paddle, canoe, and the water all dance to these predictable rules. Understanding and applying this knowledge to your canoeing technique is important to becoming a smooth, efficient paddler.

Consider Isaac Newton's three Laws of Motion. First, a body will remain at rest or in constant motion until it is acted upon by an outside force. Second, the greater the force on a body, the greater its acceleration will be. Third, for every action there is an equal and opposite reaction. In Mr. McLean's high school physics class, I struggled with formulas and figures, using stopwatches, rolling carts, and colliding balls to learn about motion. How much better this could have been explained on a pond in a canoe with paddle in hand. Not only would we have had a lot of fun, but we would have grasped the concepts immediately, establishing an instant application for this knowledge while developing a lifelong skill.

In canoeing, every stroke is an example of Newton's Laws at work. According to the Third Law, the *action* is the energy applied on the paddle blade by the canoeist. The *reaction* is the response of the water molecules in the opposite direction to the energy applied. For practical purposes, we'll say the reaction is the response of the canoe, generally in the opposite direction. It is important to keep in mind that these laws are also at work when the external force is created by a wind or waves pushing against the hull of your canoe.

Another way to understand this is to pick up a tennis racket and ball, thinking of them as the paddle blade and the water. Hit the ball straight against a wall with a consistent swing (take consistent paddle strokes). Now vary the angle of the racket head (the paddle blade). Even though the swing of the racket remains the same (the paddle stroke remains constant), it is the *pitch* of the racket head (the paddle blade) that the ball (the water) reacts to. *When you vary the angle of the blade to the water, the canoe will react by moving in the direction opposite to this angle.* (See, for example, the sculling draw in Chapter 8, The Path of the Canoe, and the sliding pry and slice in Chapter 10, U-Turns and Sideslips.)

Onside and Offside Versus Left and Right

Now conjure up an imaginary line dividing you and the canoe into two parts. The side you are holding the paddle on will be called the *onside*. Everything and every action on your onside is called your onside something (onside knee, onside gunwale, onside turn, and so on). Everything on the other side is called the *offside*. In solo canoeing, you will perform onside strokes on your onside, and cross strokes on your offside. In tandem paddling, the onside and offside reference is always based on the bow paddler's paddling side. In all cases, this avoids the terms "left" and "right," which can be very confusing.

Pick Your Paddling Side and Stick to It

There is nothing wrong with being an ambidextrous paddler. The ability to master strokes on both sides of the canoe reduces fatigue and makes you a popular tandem partner. In tandem canoeing, paddlers pick *opposite* paddling sides, with the bow paddler setting the cadence. For solo paddling it is easiest to pick your naturally strong side and stick to it. Although switching hands in the middle of maneuvers can be tempting, we encourage you to learn a more efficient way through the use of cross strokes and good technique.

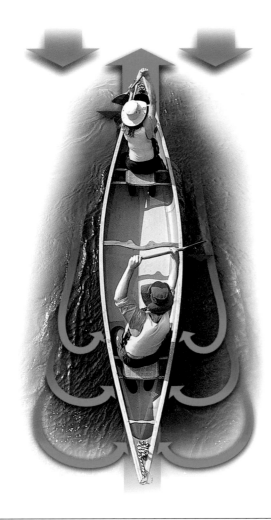

How to View the Illustrations

➡ Force of the paddle against the water

➡ Path traveled by the canoe

➡ Force of the water against the canoe or paddle

Physical Resistances that Affect the Canoe

As your canoe moves through the water there are three forms of resistance that act upon it. They are *frontal, surface,* and *eddy resistance.* Frontal and eddy resistance create very different pressures on the canoe. By understanding and working with these forces, canoeists can execute strokes in the most effective and energy-saving manner. Surface resistance is simply the friction of water molecules acting on the hull of the canoe.

Frontal resistance acts upon the *leading end* of the canoe, that is, whichever end is pushing through the water and wind. It exerts the greatest pressure on the canoe. If the canoe is going forward, then the leading end, or *frontal-resistance end,* is the bow. If going backward, it is the stern. As the canoe pushes through the water, the water presses in on each side of the canoe, providing a stabilizing effect up to its widest point (generally at the pivot point). Strokes executed at this end of the canoe are *power strokes.*

As the canoe moves through space, it displaces water and air. Beyond the canoe's widest point, a vacuum is left to be filled by an unstable swirl of air and water. This is called the *eddy-resistance end,* or *following end,* of the canoe. Since there is little water pressure being exerted on this end of the canoe, *turning and correction strokes* have the most effect here. If you are having trouble imagining this, think of your canoe as a rock in a river. The water hits the upstream (frontal-resistance) end of the rock in the same way as it hits the leading end of your canoe when it is moving through the water. The water moving behind the rock, running contrary to the main current, is the eddy; the water at the eddy-resistance end of the canoe behaves in the same way. The farther these strokes are placed away from the pivot point in the eddy-resistance end of the canoe, the easier the canoe is to turn.

The Pivot Point and a Well-Trimmed Canoe

The *pivot point* is a specific point on the bottom of the canoe where the total weight of the canoe is in balance. Since the pivot point is the point at which your canoe sinks most deeply in the water, it is the place where the canoe is initially most stable. It is also the point that most resists spinning or turning. It makes sense that in order to turn your canoe, the paddle blade should be placed as far from the pivot point as possible.

A *well-trimmed* canoe is balanced from side to side and from bow to stern. When the canoe is at rest in the water it is neither listing to one side or the other, nor is it heavier at the bow or stern. Variations in canoe design, tandem paddlers of different weights, and distribution of tripping gear can all affect the trim of the canoe. It's important to have the canoe well-trimmed so that the pivot point is on the centerline, as close to the center of the canoe as possible.

The Paddle as Anchor

1-2 *The wind-up to the catch.*

3 *The propulsion.*

4 *The exit.*

Pivot Point

5 *The recovery.*

Efficient paddling technique means not wasting your energy. When you plant the blade, you want most of that energy to be transferred to the canoe. That means the blade moves minimally. Take, for example, the forward stroke shown here. The blade is planted beside the orange marker buoy, where it remains as the canoe moves in the opposite direction.

To understand this concept better, imagine yourself kneeling on a toboggan. You are poised at the top of the hill. Reaching forward, ahead of the toboggan, anchor your hands in the snow. As you pull back, the toboggan slides forward past your hands. Consider also the double-poling action when you are cross-country skiing, planting both poles ahead of your body. Apply energy to the poles, and your body and skis are propelled past the planted poles. A planted paddle works in the same way.

Every stroke can be thought of in five phases: the *wind-up*, the *catch*, the *propulsion*, the *exit*, and the *recovery*. However, as in walking, the movement is actually one continuous fluid motion repeated again and again.

The canoe is a remarkable invention that evolved from the aboriginal peoples' need to survive on a landscape scribed with navigable waterways. It supports a load far greater than its own weight and can easily be carried alone even by a small person. Lifting the canoe requires finesse and timing, not superhuman strength.

5 The Art of Portaging

One of Gary's early memories of canoeing goes back to paddling the canoe alone for the first time. Being of small size, he would sit on the stern seat facing the stern instead of the bow as you normally would. With just a foot and a half of the canoe ahead of him, he would paddle off, pulling the rest of the craft behind him like the engineer on a train. He needed no one else to help him once he was on the water, but getting the canoe to the water or going beyond the bounds of Rabbit Lake was another thing. Then one summer when he was big enough, he began practicing the art of portaging.

Gary discovered that if he picked up the stern end of the canoe, leaving the bow to rest on the ground, he could flip it over his head. He could then walk up its length, bouncing his hands along the gunwales until the portage yoke was centered over his shoulders. At this point, he tipped the bow up off the ground so that the entire craft was balanced on his shoulders. As long as the canoe was perfectly balanced from stern to bow, he found he could carry it short distances. That feeling was as sweet and memorable as balancing on a bicycle for the very first time.

One day, Gary's father took him to Rabbit Creek to paddle the remaining distance to the lake. A pair of foxes, one silver, one gray, watched him pass on the first riverbend as he headed downstream through the steep-sided valley. The river was full of twists and turns, and he came to a logjam just before the entrance to Rabbit Lake. Putting the newly discovered technique to use, he picked the canoe up and carried it around the barrier, making one stop along the trail to rest the bow in the crook of a tree. By the time he reached Rabbit Lake, the initiation marked a new era of personal exploration. He felt he could now go anywhere.

For the most part, we find walking solo with a canoe easier and safer than a tandem carry. You can more easily maneuver between trees and around other obstructions while moving at your own pace. A tandem portage is sometimes preferable, as when crossing open ground on a windy day, or negotiating a very steep embankment, or if the weight of the canoe is simply unmanageable for one. It makes an enormous difference to have a contoured and preferably well-padded portage yoke that is positioned in the canoe so that the canoe is perfectly balanced side to side and fore to aft.

Being a person of small proportions has its advantages. I have had to learn the art of leverage and good technique because big muscles have never been there to save the day. Unless the canoe is a very heavy, awkward beast, portaging merely requires finesse and timing.

You can pick up and put down the canoe with equal control by yourself. Use the one-person lift shown in these photos. The same procedure shown for picking up and putting down a canoe alone also works for a tandem portage. Partners stand on the same side of the canoe at opposite ends, with the bow paddler just forward of the bow seat and the stern paddler just aft of the stern seat. It helps to count "One, two, three!" before lifting. (Make sure you walk in the direction the bow is facing.) Once the canoe is swung overhead, the bow paddler places the deck of the canoe on one shoulder. This gives him an unobstructed view. If you are carrying the stern, step back a bit until the gunwales are close enough together to rest on both shoulders. In a tandem carry it helps to have the tallest person carry the bow.

If it is a short distance to the water, the campsite, or over the beaver dam, the canoe can be carried like a suitcase, right side up with paddlers on opposite sides, one person at the bow and the other at the stern. Each paddler lifts the canoe by means of the carrying thwarts located at bow and stern.

Lifting the Canoe

1 Stand up straight, with your legs slightly apart and knees bent. Grasp the gunwale at the center thwart. Your fingers are inside the gunwale and your thumbs are outside the gunwale.

2 Keeping your back straight and your legs bent, lift the canoe to your thighs with a rocking motion.

3 Grasp the center thwart with the stern-facing hand (in this case, my left hand). Pull the canoe up and toward you, keeping this arm straight.

4 Reach across the whole width of the canoe grasping the far gunwale with the bow-facing hand (in this case, my right hand). Your fingers are out and your thumb is in. Change your near-gunwale grip so that your fingers are out and your thumb is in.

5 With one smooth motion, swing the canoe up and over your head. Begin straightening your legs as you step around 90 degrees to face the bow.

6 Ideally, you have a padded, contoured yoke at the center thwart so the canoe can rest comfortably on your shoulders. The canoe's weight should be balanced side to side and bow to stern. This makes for a more pleasant carry.

Putting the Canoe Down

1 Putting the canoe down is picking it up in reverse, except gravity helps. The canoe should be resting at balance on your shoulders with your arms merely providing stability during the carry.

2 Bend your knees then straighten them while simultaneously straightening your arms. Raise the canoe up and away as you step 90 degrees to one side. Bend your knees to absorb the canoe's weight.

3 In a smooth, controlled fashion, lower the canoe to your thighs.

4 Grasp the center thwart with the stern-facing (left) hand. Then let go of the outside gunwale and grab the near gunwale with the right hand, fingers inside the gunwale and your thumb outside.

5 Let go of the center thwart and grasp the near gunwale, fingers in and thumb out. Roll the canoe down to the ground.

6 Setting a canoe down with quiet control has its advantages in many circumstances. Whether at the river's edge or along a rocky lakeshore, you are less likely to cause injury to yourself or your faithful craft.

Down by the water's edge on Lake Superior's east shore, we set up camp facing west. The tent and canoe are resting on Canadian Shield granite. The last great glaciers smoothed the bedrock and boulders to their present polished appearance.

6 Flatwater: The Paddler's Magic Carpet

One summer we circumnavigated Lake Superior by canoe. Located at the height of North America's Great Lakes, Superior is the largest expanse of fresh water on Earth. There were times when the lake was a gigantic mirror reflecting the old mountain shapes, sunset colors, and starry nights. Then, we were on a "flatwater journey." But there were many times when this freshwater ocean was anything but flat. We encountered seiches, small, tide-like movements, that caused the water to ebb and flow in between the lake's islands, creating river features like eddies, haystacks, and whirlpools. And when we encountered crosswinds and rolling seas on open traverses, we had to apply all the canoeing skills we possessed to safely reach shore.

Even if you never plan to paddle on Lake Superior or run whitewater rapids, embracing the techniques and skills in this book will stand you in good stead while, for instance, bucking a headwind on a big lake. On trips where you never plan to run moving water, the art of an efficient forward stroke can help you paddle much more easily into a wind, especially in a solo canoe.

This book is laid out in a learning progression of maneuvers and strokes. Follow them and you will build a strong foundation of efficient canoeing technique from the very first time you pick up a paddle and step into a canoe. Many of the following demonstrations were photographed on a bay in Temagami where Gary first learned to swim and canoe. In summer the water is clean, warm, shallow, and protected from the winds. If you can be selective about your flatwater paddling site, do so. Wind makes it harder to learn proper technique on flatwater.

We will be looking at three categories of maneuvers and strokes, beginning with those most easily accomplished. First, in Chapter 7, Getting Centered, are the righting strokes, which are used to prevent the canoe from tipping to the onside or offside. Confidence-building exercises like "Rock the Boat" reinforce the basic principles of body movement. Following these, in Chapter 8, The Path of the Canoe, are the turning and corrective strokes and maneuvers. Canoes have a natural tendency to turn, so these strokes meet with much success even on a canoeist's first attempt. The third category of strokes and maneuvers is more challenging; these keep the canoe going in a straight line, and are described in Chapter 9, Moving Forward, and Chapter 10, Moving Backward.

A word about strokes and maneuvers. The dictionary defines a *stroke* as "one complete performance of a recurrent action or movement." A paddle stroke is exactly that, the complete movement of paddler, paddle, and canoe — not, as one might think, a single action of the paddle blade. That fluidity of movement and the connection of one action to another leads us to *maneuvers*.

As you follow along, you will notice that we always refer first to the maneuvers being performed and then to the specific strokes used. It is important to think of what you want to accomplish. Think of *sideslipping* past a rock, making a *U-turn* around a stump, or *spinning* the canoe to face in another direction.

Launching the Canoe

Getting in and out of a canoe can be awkward for novice paddlers, and we have seen our share of unintentional swims. Most have been funny for both spectators and swimmers, however, cold-water dunkings, drowned cameras, soaked wallets, damaged equipment, and bruised pride have led us to show these maneuvers in more detail.

To learn to launch with finesse, find a suitable launching site; a dock or a shallow sand beach without waves is good. To avoid the common and embarrassing mistake of getting into the canoe backward, decide upon launching which end is bow and stern. The stern seat is set closer to the end of the canoe, while the bow seat provides more space for the paddler's legs.

Whenever you are getting in the canoe, make sure you keep your weight low and over the centerline. Spread the paddle across the gunwales for stability. Place the blade toward your paddling side. A solo paddler can launch a canoe in the same way.

Over the years, some of our favorite canoeing has been along winding creeks such as the West Aubinadong. You never know what to expect around the next bend; it could be a bittern in the bullrushes, a moose, a beaver at work on a dam, or a huge fallen pine over which you will have to pull the canoe.

Launching from a Dock

1 *Don lifejackets and have paddles ready. Pick the canoe up amidships and lower it hand-over-hand into the water, to a position perpendicular to the dock.*

2 *The stern paddler swings the canoe parallel to the dock (bow facing into the wind if there is any). Since the bow has more buoyancy, the bow paddler gets in first while the stern paddler steadies the canoe.*

3 *From a crouched position on the dock, the bow paddler steadies the bow end by holding the paddle shaft across the gunwales, with the blade extended toward her paddling side. She steps in, keeping her weight over the centerline of the canoe.*

4 *The bow paddler kneels, holding her paddle in the ready position. The stern paddler steadies the canoe by spreading his paddle across the gunwales, blade on his paddling side, all the while holding the dock. He steps in, keeping his balance over the centerline.*

5 *Once the stern paddler is also in the ready position, you are set to move smoothly away from the dock.*

Launching from Shore

At the end of the portage trail, your paddling partner motions toward a bay nearby where a velvet-antlered moose is feeding. Quietly you slide the canoe in hand over hand. The bow paddler gets in first, then the stern paddler pushes off from shore without so much as a bump or a ripple. This art of getting in the canoe gracefully has its advantages, not least of which are safety for paddlers and ease on equipment.

Demonstrated here are two ways to launch from shore: the *bow-first launch* and the *broadside launch*. When you are getting into the canoe, it should be completely afloat for stability. For a broadside launch, you may have to get your feet wet. If there isn't enough room to pull the canoe in sideways, place the bow facing out perpendicular to shore. The bow-first method also works well in waves or wind.

The Bow-First Launch

1 Set the canoe at right angles to shore when there is not enough shoreline to allow you to pull the canoe in sideways. On a windy day the canoe can be faced directly into the waves.

2 The stern paddler holds the canoe while the bow paddler walks up the length of the canoe along the centerline. Maintain stability by spreading your paddle shaft across the gunwales and keep your weight low.

3 The bow paddler sits or kneels and places the paddle in the ready position. The stern paddler holds the paddle shaft across the gunwales for stability.

4 The stern paddler slides his paddle forward along the gunwales, continuing to hold both paddle shaft and gunwales. The blade is positioned on the side opposite to the bow paddler's paddling side.

5 With the stern paddler kneeling, paddle in the ready position, you are ready to go.

The Broadside Launch

1 *A calm day on a sandy shoreline provides the easiest launch. This is a simple but important technique tandem paddlers can use to avoid an unfortunate capsize along the river shoreline.*

2 *The bow paddler keeps her weight low, bracing with the paddle shaft spread across the gunwales. Once the bow paddler is seated, the stern paddler gets in. Make sure your paddle blades are placed on opposite sides of the canoe in the ready position.*

3 *On a calm lake, the stern paddler can push away from shore as he steps in. However if you are leaving shore with a river current flowing past, it is advisable for both paddlers to be kneeling with blades in the water before pushing off.*

4 *With both paddlers kneeling, paddles in the ready position on opposite sides of the canoe, the tandem team is ready to head out.*

Many Happy Landings

Every canoeist should practice smooth, polished landings. Broadside landings are preferable to bow-first landings. The abeam, U-turn, and sideslip maneuvers referred to here will be learned in Chapters 8 and 10.

Paddle straight toward shore and, when about two canoe-lengths away, make a U-turn until you are parallel to the shore. Move smoothly sideways with an abeam. The stern paddler gets out first, reversing the steps of the broadside launching.

Coming ashore where there is room only for a bow-first landing also requires a cautious approach so as not to ram into the dock, rocks, or shore.

The bow paddler steadies herself while holding her paddle shaft across the gunwales. She steps forward onto the shore, while the stern paddler steadies the canoe in the ready position. With the bow stem just resting onshore, the bow paddler holds the canoe steady. Moving his paddle forward along the gunwales, the stern paddler walks along the centerline and gets out at the bow. The bow-first method also works well if there are waves or wind.

7 Getting Centered

One of our first big physical challenges in life is learning to walk. We master this art of balancing in motion simply by trying and trying again, learning the forces of gravity until the skill becomes as natural as breathing. As we grow older, a variety of activities give us an intuitive sense of the laws of motion. Comprehending how these forces act upon us is not the point. We just do it.

Our parents ran with us as we balanced on bicycles until one day we just took off on our own. In winter they'd hold our hands until our ice skates no longer slithered out from beneath us. We skied with friends down steep slopes, over jumps, and through slalom courses. And when it came to paddling, it was by playing that we discovered the limits of our equipment and skills. This meant going out with the intent of tipping the canoe over. We would fill the canoes up with water and, fully submerged, try paddling them to shore with our hands. We would wear dive masks and flip over to look around at the underwater world. The air pocket under the overturned canoe was a secret cave and a place for making plans. The overturned hull was a diving platform. On hot days, we swam for hours and hours under, over, and around the canoe, pushing it, pulling it, swamping it. The canoe was, in short, an agreeable friend that would do anything we wanted it to. We hope that this book encourages you to approach canoeing with that same sense of fun.

Rock the Boat

1   "Rock the Boat" will assure you that it is not the canoe that is tippy, but merely your lack of balance that makes it so. Use your knees to rock the canoe from edge to edge while keeping your upper body upright. Rock the canoe quickly then slowly, and then hold the edge for a few moments on each side.

2   Hold your paddles overhead, using only the weighting of one knee and the unweighting of the other to edge the canoe from side to side. This means stretching one side of your body (and weighting that knee) while kinking the other side of your body (and unweighting that knee). Rock the Boat develops balance and is essential for good canoeing technique.

J-Leaning Your Body and Edging the Canoe

When you *J-lean your body*, you are *edging the canoe*. When we wish to put the canoe on its edge for a turn, or to "raise the side of opposition," as in sideslipping and abeams, we refer to *edging* the canoe, in the same way we think of edging our skis. To edge the canoe to the left, the left side of your body is stretched and the right side of your body is kinked. Vice versa, to edge the canoe to the right, the right side of your body is stretched and the left side kinked. *Your upper body remains upright over your balance point.*

Throughout this book, we refrain from using the word "leaning" in the context of the canoe because, in our experience, the word is interpreted as "leaning the body" instead of "leaning the canoe."

In edging the canoe, the lower half of your body is adopting the shape of a J, or an inverted J, by pushing down and weighting one knee and unweighting and lifting the other. Think of the chines on a canoe in the same way as you think of the edges of your skis or skates. Whether in a canoe or on skis or skates, you weight the inside edge to turn.

The Kneeling Ready Position

In the *kneeling ready position,* your knees are spread wide to increase stability. Your weight is distributed between your buttocks and your knees. It is easier to rotate your upper body and edge the canoe when you are kneeling. The seat on your canoe should be placed high enough to allow your feet to rest comfortably beneath it without being wedged in or pressed sideways but, at the same time, low enough that your buttocks fall comfortably against the edge of the seat without creating an awkward stretch.

When you are not doing anything else with your paddle, it should be in the *ready position.* Place the blade parallel to the canoe's centerline beside your hip. Both arms are relaxed and your hands are over the water with the control thumb back. This is called the ready position because you are ready to right yourself or take a stroke. In the event of a sudden tip, beginning canoeists often grab the gunwales hoping for support. But the force applied to the gunwales actually pulls the canoe over faster. Instead, use the righting strokes. If you rotate your body to your onside and apply a little force to the powerface in the ready position, you are in the *high brace position.* This is useful for recovering from slight tips to the offside.

The Sitting Ready Position

One advantage canoeing has over kayaking is that you can alter your paddling position on long stretches of open water, lakes, and quiet rivers. Although kneeling provides the greatest relief for your back and spine, you will find that sitting gives your knees and legs a rest. However, instead of stretching your legs straight out in front of you, bend them, letting your knees fall outward toward the gunwales. By tucking one leg under the seat, you can increase your stability. You are also ready to drop into the kneeling position should you need to lower your center of gravity quickly.

Righting Strokes

Recovering your balance can be a simple matter of putting exaggerated pressure on the backface or powerface of the paddle. However, the righting pry and low brace maneuvers, demonstrated here, address situations in which you need to make a radical recovery to prevent a capsize. Recovering from that point of no return requires a quick response. You should be able to react by feel, not by thought, instinctively setting up a righting pry or low brace when that wave hits you suddenly out of nowhere. The trick with recovery is lots of practice and surprise exercises to improve your reflexes. Performing these maneuvers in a solo canoe teaches you that you are responsible for the moves you make. By mastering the righting pry and the low brace, you do more than keep yourself upright; you build the confidence necessary to execute any maneuver properly.

The *righting pry* is truly a stroke of commitment. When executed properly, it is amazing how this stroke will prevent a capsize to the offside. (It is helpful to review what we have to say about the high brace position on page 39.) To practice, place your paddle in the ready position. Rotate your shoulders so that they are in line with the canoe's centerline. Slice the paddle toward your hip, keeping the shaft vertical. (Set the shaft against the gunwale with an open hand to keep from pinching your fingers between the gunwale and paddle shaft.) Turn your control thumb back so that the powerface faces the canoe. At this point, it is essential to push down on the grip so that the blade is

Righting Pry

1 From the ready position, edge the canoe to your offside as if you are tipping in that direction. With your control thumb pointing out, slice the paddle toward your hip, making sure the blade is well under the hull and the shaft is set against the gunwale.

2 Point your control thumb back, thereby twisting the paddle's powerface so that it is parallel with the canoe's centerline. In order to drive the blade deep when your onside is elevated, you must slide your shaft hand up the shaft (choke up).

3 Pull the grip aggressively toward the offside gunwale past the centerline by using the power of your upper body. Twist your torso to face forward, keeping your control arm relatively straight and horizontal.

4 The righting pry happens very quickly and, if done properly, is extremely effective the first time. Although a second righting pry is seldom necessary, if needed, it must follow up on the first one immediately.

driven deep into the water. Pull the grip toward you by unwinding your torso and keeping your control arm relatively straight and horizontal throughout. The righting pry is very effective in preventing capsizes to the offside.

The *low brace* prevents tipping to the onside (the side you are paddling on). The degree to which you perform a low brace depends on whether it is being used to correct a minor tip or a point-of-no-return tip. The technique shown here is for the latter example and it is even used in the final stages of the open canoe roll (see pages 134–135 and 176–177). Rotate your upper body so that the plane of your shoulders is in line with the

canoe's centerline. Turn your control thumb out so that when you brace you will hit the water with the backface of the paddle. With the paddle shaft horizontal, the knuckles on both hands will be out over the water and getting wet when you perform the brace. (Both arms will have a slight bend.)

Now tip the canoe toward your onside until you are on the verge of capsizing. The low brace takes place beside and in front of your body, with three things happening all at once. First of all, arch your back and brace by hitting the water with your entire paddle. Second, throw your head toward the blade and keep looking down. (This is an example of Newton's

Third Law, the action-reaction law. By throwing your head down, you create a force in the opposite direction, that is, a force that will help you right the canoe.) The third thing is to unweight your onside knee and weight your offside knee. Concentrate on weighting this offside knee instead of putting weight on your paddle. Sweep the blade toward the bow, following the motion with your body. (The blade is on a slight climbing angle.) Lean forward, bringing your upper body across the centerline, and keep your head down throughout because lifting it will negate what you are doing with the rest of your body.

Low Brace

1 *Edge to your onside and twist your upper body to face the water. Hold the paddle horizontal with your control thumb facing forward.*

2 *The paddle shaft is horizontal and perpendicular to the canoe's centerline. The backface hits the water on a climbing angle at the same time as do both hands, knuckles down. At the same time, arch your back and throw your head forward.*

3 *Put pressure on your offside knee. Unweight your onside knee while lightly bracing on the paddle. Sweep the blade toward the bow. Follow the blade with your upper body, rotating your onside shoulder forward. Keep your head down until your upper body passes the canoe's centerline.*

Solo or Tandem?

We have described maneuvers from two viewpoints, that of the solo canoeist and that of a canoeist paddling in tandem with another. Whether you are a novice or a seasoned paddler, there is much to be learned in a solo canoe. By understanding how your own actions have the power to influence the movements of the canoe, you also become a much better tandem paddler.

Gary and I have been paddling canoes together for as long as we have known one another, but we have also paddled kayaks and solo canoes, and we have found a great benefit in a balance of experiences. Tandem canoeing offers the shared excitement of a sport where your individual effort is complemented by another's. It is the companionship of sharing experiences in the places that only canoes can take you. If you are starting out together in a tandem canoe, especially as a couple, it is a good idea to keep an open mind. You have adopted these new appendages, and it will take a little time before you move with grace.

Positive communication between paddling partners greatly simplifies things. We find that giving instructions — "sweep, sweep, draw, draw" — meets with less success than suggesting the maneuver, "Let's spin the canoe to the onside." Teamwork is the key.

Some of the finest paddling in the world is found among Lake Superior's northern islands between Nipigon and Rossport. We have spent weeks poking along this volcanic rock shoreline, which has been carved into caves and arches and studded with agate and amethyst gems.

Righting Strokes for the Tandem Canoe

Practice your righting strokes in comfortable conditions, ideally when the air and water temperature is above 70°F (20°C), because capsizes are likely. If you must practice your righting strokes when the air or water are cold, dress for it in a wetsuit or drysuit. If this isn't possible, then practice them at the end of a paddling session. Another solution is to join a canoe club and rent some time in the public swimming pool over the winter. This way, you can also perfect your canoe roll in controlled conditions.

Now that you have accomplished both righting strokes paddling solo, it is time to try them with a paddling partner. To prevent a cap-size in a tandem canoe, one paddler uses a low brace and the other paddler uses a righting pry. The strokes provide double the power to right the canoe if they are performed in unison. It is easiest to first develop good reflexes for these strokes while in a solo canoe. If the canoe is tipping to the offside, as shown in these photos, the stern paddler performs a low brace and the bow paddler uses a righting pry. If the capsize is going to the onside, the bow paddler executes a low brace and the stern paddler, the righting pry. By having both paddlers react in the same way that they would if paddling solo, there is the greatest opportunity for preventing capsize.

If you have a third paddling friend along, get her to stand at the stern of the canoe in shallow water. Have her tip it suddenly one way or the other. You will not know what is going to happen so this is a great exercise, mimicking the conditions under which righting strokes are used. You always need them when you least expect to. Good reflexes are fun to develop alone or with a partner. (This particular exercise is shown in Chapter 16, Balancing for the River, on page 133.) For a tandem team, these exercises teach us that whether we paddle bow or stern, we each take responsibility for keeping the canoe upright.

1 Both the stern and bow paddlers can assist in avoiding capsize. In this demonstration, the canoe is tipped to the offside. The stern paddler uses a low brace and the bow paddler, a righting pry.

2 The strokes are performed in unison. The bow paddler chokes up, thrusts the paddle blade deep down into the water, and yanks on the grip at the same time as the stern paddler slaps the horizontal paddle down in the low brace and sweeps it forward.

3 Both paddlers unwind their upper bodies to end up facing forward. The canoe is brought back to an upright position with both paddlers in the ready position. Practice your righting strokes by tipping the canoe to both sides.

8 The Path of the Canoe

Remember that *strokes* are performed with the paddle, while *maneuvers* are what happens to the canoe. Repeated strokes or combinations of different strokes result in canoe maneuvers. The strokes and maneuvers described in this chapter are useful in turning the canoe and in correcting its course.

Solo Offside Spin Using the Forward Sweep

Sweep strokes are used to *spin* the canoe on its pivot point without any forward or backward movement of the canoe. A smooth transition between each phase of the stroke is essential. Although the blade appears to make a 180-degree arc from bow to stern, this is an illusion. *It is the canoe that moves.* The canoe is spinning around its own pivot point like a pinwheel. Remember the principle of the paddle as an anchor, as described in Chapter 4. *The paddle blade hardly moves at all.*

To initiate the *forward sweep*, lean forward from the hips, rotating your onside shoulder forward. Your hands are low and over the water. The paddle shaft is nearly horizontal. Turn your control thumb up so that the paddle blade is vertical. Place the blade as close to the canoe's centerline as possible. Your onside knee is weighted so that as the bow swings to the offside (away from the blade), there is less resistance against the hull. As you apply pressure to the blade, the canoe begins to spin.

Follow the paddle shaft by unwinding your torso. (Keeping your eyes on the blade throughout the sweep will help you to completely rotate your torso.) When the blade reaches your hip, transfer your weight to your offside knee and lean back slightly. This offside edging and more heavily weighted stern allows the canoe to spin to the blade with less resistance. The plane of your shoulders remains parallel to the paddle shaft throughout. Bring the stern to the blade without letting them touch. Both hands will be over the water. Turn your control thumb forward.

With a quick, clean exit, feather the blade back across the surface of the water with a slight climbing angle. (A *climbing angle* means that the leading edge of the blade is angled upward, so if the blade accidentally catches the surface it will bounce into the air instead of catching water and diving.) Plant the paddle, apply pressure, and spin again.

1 *Choke up with the shaft hand. Bend forward from the hips and rotate your onside shoulder toward the bow. With a low shaft-angle, anchor the blade as close to the canoe's centerline as possible.*

2 *Your control thumb is turned up, which means the blade is vertical in the water. Apply force to the powerface. Unwind your upper body, keeping your shoulders aligned with the paddle shaft.*

3 *Follow the blade with your eyes. When the blade is perpendicular to the hull, your upper body will be in an upright position with your weight evenly balanced.*

4 *Continue to rotate your onside shoulder back through the last half of the stroke. Lean back slightly and weight the offside knee. The canoe pivots until the stern almost meets the paddle blade.*

5 *In one smooth motion, turn the control thumb forward and feather the blade back to the bow. Your eyes and shoulders should follow the line of the paddle shaft as your weight is shifted to the onside knee once again.*

6 *Feather the blade all the way back to the bow. That means the blade slices through the air or water with one edge of the blade leading so there is minimal resistance. Turn the control thumb up, anchor the blade, and repeat.*

Solo Onside Spin Using the Reverse Sweep

Begin setting up the *reverse sweep* by rotating your torso until the plane of your shoulders is parallel to the canoe's centerline. Both hands are over the water, holding the paddle shaft horizontal. (Remember to choke up with the shaft hand so that the blade is as far from the pivot point as possible.) The blade angle and the blade face are different for the reverse sweep and the forward sweep. During the reverse sweep, the blade is on a 45-degree climbing angle instead of a vertical 90 degrees, and pressure is applied to the blade's backface instead of the powerface.

Rotate your onside shoulder forward, keeping your shoulder plane in line with the paddle shaft. Follow the blade with your eyes. Once again you want to concentrate on edging the canoe so that it spins easier. At the beginning of the stroke, the stern is spinning away from the blade, so weight your onside knee to lift the canoe's offside. By the time the blade is at your hip, your torso is in an upright position. Shift your weight to your offside knee to allow the bow to continue spinning toward the anchored paddle blade. Once the blade is at the bow and as close to the centerline as possible, make a quick, clean exit from the water. Your control thumb turns back as the blade feathers back, just skimming the surface before anchoring again for another sweep.

It is important to remember to keep the shaft angle low and to extend the blade as far from the pivot point as possible. Edge the canoe onside in the first half of the sweep and edge the canoe offside in the second half of the sweep.

Some strokes call for raising the shaft hand up the shaft away from the throat of the paddle. This is called choking up on the paddle. During a sweep stroke, this technique enables a paddler to get the blade as far from the pivot point as possible. In the case of the righting pry, this prevents finger pinching and allows the blade to be well submerged.

1 Twist your upper body so that your shoulders are close to parallel with the canoe's centerline. Choke up on the paddle shaft and establish a low shaft-angle as you anchor the blade as close to the hull as possible.

2 Weight the onside knee. Apply force to the blade, keeping the backface of the blade on a 45-degree climbing angle to the surface. Keep your shoulders in line with the paddle shaft. Watch the blade with your eyes. The canoe is turning around its pivot point.

3 The further the blade is extended from the canoe's pivot point, the more easily the canoe spins. Pressure is exerted on the backface of the paddle blade during the reverse sweep.

4 As the blade passes your hip, begin edging the canoe to the offside by weighting the offside knee. Note how the blade remains stationary as the canoe swings around its pivot point.

5 The bow swings toward the blade but, just before they meet, the blade exits the water (with your control thumb pointing back). Feather the blade back, keeping the shaft low. While recovering the blade, rotate your upper body back to repeat the stroke.

Tandem Onside Spin Using Sweeps

Spinning the canoe using forward and reverse sweeps is the quickest and most efficient way to reposition the canoe to face in another direction. To spin the canoe to the onside, follow the demonstration shown here. To spin the canoe to the offside, see pages 50–51.

To perform an *onside spin* in a tandem canoe using sweep strokes, the bow and stern paddlers do their *quarter sweeps* in unison. The bow paddler begins by rotating her torso toward the onside gunwale for a *reverse quarter sweep*. Plant the blade straight out from your hip with a low shaft-angle. Apply force to the blade. Rotate your onside shoulder forward. The bow spins toward the blade. When the bow reaches the blade, turn your control thumb back. Lift the blade cleanly from the water, feathering it back on a climbing angle. Plant the paddle out from your hip and repeat.

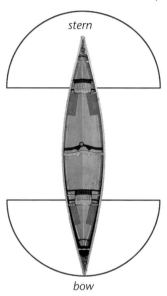

stern

bow

The stern paddler's *forward quarter sweep*, commonly referred to as a *stern sweep*, complements the bow paddler's reverse quarter sweep. The forward quarter sweep resembles the second part of the solo paddler's forward sweep. The blade starts out at the stern paddler's hip and ends at the stern of the canoe. Follow the blade and rotate your onside shoulder back. Plant the blade vertically, apply pressure, and spin the canoe until the blade almost, but not quite, touches the stern. Turn your control thumb forward, then feather the blade forward. Plant the paddle blade and repeat.

Rhythm is the key to smooth spinning. Practice your spins by doing several 360-degree revolutions without stopping.

1   *The bow paddler sets up a reverse quarter sweep toward the bow while the stern paddler sets up a stern sweep to the stern. Both paddles are perpendicular to the canoe.*

2   *Keeping in mind the paddler's box, the canoeists rotate their upper bodies, following the sweep toward the ends of the canoe. Perform sweeps in unison for smooth spins.*

3   *Force is exerted on the backface of the bow paddler's blade and on the powerface of the stern paddler's blade. Both blades remain almost stationary while the canoe spins.*

4   *At the end of the propulsion phase, the bow paddler feathers her blade back by turning her control thumb back. Simultaneously, the stern paddler turns his control thumb forward and feathers the blade forward.*

5   *At the end of the recovery, both paddlers are ready to set up for the next sweep. The tandem canoe, unlike a solo canoe, is kept level during the spin.*

Tandem Offside Spin Using Sweeps

In order to spin the tandem canoe to the offside using sweeps, the bow paddler uses a forward quarter sweep and the stern paddler uses a reverse quarter sweep. (This spin is the opposite of the tandem spin shown on pages 48–49.) Paddle placement at the beginning of the sweep stroke is, as always, important. The idea is to get the force as far from the pivot point as possible.

To begin the spin, the blades are placed as close to the centerline as possible. The bow paddler rotates the onside shoulder forward. The stern paddler rotates back, placing both hands over the water with the paddle shaft horizontal. Both paddlers submerge their blades; the bow paddler's is vertical and the stern paddler's is on a climbing angle. In unison, both paddlers rotate their torsos until their paddles are perpendicular to the canoe's centerline.

Keep both arms relatively straight. This is important for two reasons. First of all, the muscle power will be generated by the big torso muscles rather than the arms; and second, straighter arms allow for a greater reach from the pivot point.

At the end of the quarter sweep, rather than lifting the paddle, think of turning your control thumb in the direction that you wish to return the blade to. Point your control thumb forward to feather the blade forward in the bow; to feather the blade back in the stern, point your control thumb back.

It is also useful to keep in mind that, unlike a solo canoe, the tandem canoe is kept level throughout the spin.

1 Plant both blades as close to the centerline of the canoe as possible. Choke up with the shaft hand and keep a low shaft-angle to achieve the greatest reach from the pivot point.

2 Both blades are fully submerged. Simultaneously apply force to the blades and rotate your upper bodies. The blades remain stationary as the canoe spins around its pivot point.

3 Once both paddles are perpendicular to the canoe, the recovery begins. Keep in mind the paddler's box. The force applied to the blade originates from the torso and back, not from the arms.

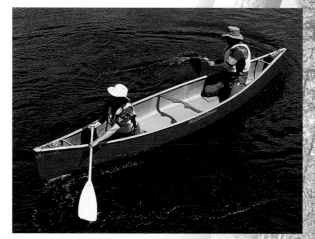

4 The bow paddler turns her control thumb forward and the stern paddler turns his control thumb back. The blades are feathered back in the direction of the paddler's control thumb, on a slight climbing angle.

A silver morning on the Mississagi River encourages us to break camp slowly. We bake bannock bread with blueberries, catch up on our travel journals, and read Grey Owl's accounts of traveling this historic route between Temagami, Biscotasing, and Lake Huron.

For three months we sought out a canoe route through Northern Ontario that would link together the remaining Great Lakes–St. Lawrence ancient forest landscapes. These places where the forest extends far beyond the lakeshore, undivided by roads, where only the sounds of nature are heard, are rare, precious, and disappearing fast.

Solo Onside Abeam Using the Draw

Remember the efficient canoeing rule, "the canoe moves, not the paddle." Let's take the draw as an example. You are not drawing the paddle to the canoe, you are drawing the canoe to the paddle. In a solo canoe (shown here), the draw is happening opposite the canoe's pivot point, resulting in a maneuver called an abeam. When these same draws are performed in a tandem canoe simultaneously at bow and stern, the resultant maneuver is another spin, as you will see on page 61.

While following this sequence, it helps to keep the following points in mind. In order to plant the paddle about 2 feet (60 cm) from the canoe with a vertical shaft, begin by weighting the onside knee and get your control hand out over the water. The water presents quite a force against which to move the canoe laterally, so it is necessary to raise the *side of opposition* by weighting the offside knee. (The side of opposition is the side of the canoe experiencing greater water pressure at any given time. If the side of opposition is not raised, the canoe's movement is slowed.) Putting this all together, the drawing action involves quickly shifting your weight from the onside to the offside knee as you rotate your upper body to face forward. The Rock the Boat exercise (see Chapter 7), edging the canoe from side to side, is really useful practice for this.

In the series shown here, the draw moves the canoe laterally without traveling forward or backward or spinning. During the underwater recovery, your control thumb must point straight out. In this way, the blade slices straight out to anchor right opposite the canoe's pivot point.

1 Rotate your shoulders toward the onside gunwale. Keep your arms comfortably straight. Stack your hands over the water with the shaft vertical and the paddle's powerface turned toward you.

2 Plant the blade opposite your pivot point to avoid spinning the canoe. Pull your hips to the anchored paddle blade by unwinding your torso and weighting your offside knee to raise the side of opposition.

3 Your upper body, acting as one unit with the paddle, unwinds toward the bow. Just before the blade touches the hull, turn your control thumb out to initiate the recovery. The powerface faces the stern.

4 The recovery is performed underwater, keeping the blade at right angles to the canoe, the shaft still vertical, and your hands stacked over the water. The blade is sliced straight out from your hip.

5 At the end of the recovery phase, turn your control thumb back, turning the powerface toward the canoe. You will then be in the "catch" position and ready to pull your hips to the anchored blade in another draw.

Solo Offside Abeam Using the Pry

A *pry* is a short, quick stroke that uses the paddle shaft as a lever against the canoe gunwale to provide force to the paddle blade. It is an easy stroke to learn once you think of your shaft hand as an oarlock anchoring the paddle shaft to the gunwale. It is helpful to lean back a little while performing this stroke. Pull the control hand only as far as the centerline and no further, or else you begin lifting water. Abeams become inefficient when the canoe tips back and forth.

Use pries in a solo canoe as a way to move your canoe sideways to your offside while keeping your blade on the onside. When pries are used simultaneously by the bow and stern paddlers in a tandem canoe, the result is another kind of spin. It is good to keep in mind that pry strokes can be made anywhere along the side of the canoe as far forward or aft as you can reach with the paddle. When the pry is performed at the bow, the canoe turns to the offside. When the pry is performed near the stern, the canoe turns to the onside. This is demonstrated in the more advanced maneuver of the sliding pry, shown on pages 84–85.

1 *Begin by rotating your upper body to face the onside gunwale. Place the powerface of the paddle blade against the hull, holding the shaft against the gunwale as if it were an oarlock. It is best to use pressure to hold it there and keep your fingers above the gunwale.*

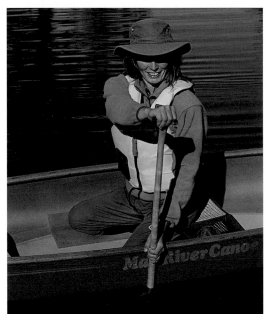

2   *Your control hand is extended a bit further out over the water than the shaft hand. (Your control thumb points back.) Pull the grip (your control hand) across your chest as you quickly unwind your upper body.*

3   *Unwind your torso quickly, facing forward, but don't let your control hand cross the centerline. Keep the shaft anchored against the gunwale, then turn your control thumb out and slice the blade back under the canoe.*

4   *Turn your control thumb back, setting your powerface against the canoe ready for another pry. Since the pry forces the onside gunwale down, it naturally keeps the side of opposition elevated.*

Solo Abeams Using Sculling and Cross Sculling Draws

Imagine yourself spreading thick icing on a three-layer cake. In order to evenly distribute the icing, you would perform somewhat the same action with your knife as you will with your paddle while *sculling*.

Sculling moves your canoe more gracefully than pulsating draws. Another way to understand the sculling action is to extend your arm out horizontally with your palm flat and facing down. Pretend you are treading water by sweeping your hand back and forth across the surface. Place your paddle grip in your onside armpit and hold the paddle shaft with the shaft hand. Continue the treading-water action with your arm outstretched. Now hold the paddle with your control hand on the grip, and continue this action. Raise your control hand until the paddle shaft is vertical and the blade is in the water. You are tracing an elongated figure eight in the water with the paddle blade.

If you find your canoe beginning to spin rather than moving laterally, you can try performing the stroke a little further forward or a little further back. The stroke has to happen right opposite the pivot point, which varies from canoe to canoe. Keep an even pressure on the blade as you trace the figure eight. The blade pitch for optimum sculling efficiency varies. If it is opened up too much, then the canoe moves back and forth as well as sideways. If it is too tight an angle, then the blade is just slicing the water and the canoe is not moving sideways. Remember to stay within the paddler's box by rotating your shoulder plane and keeping your arms comfortably straight. Abeams are much more effective when you raise your side of opposition.

In the sculling draw, force applied to the powerface results in an onside abeam. If you want to do an offside abeam, there are two possibilities: a sculling pry, where you apply force to the backface of the blade, or a cross sculling draw (as shown on the facing page).

Solo Abeam Using Sculling Draws

1 Rotate toward your onside. Stack your hands over the water with a high shaft-angle. The leading edge of the blade is no more than 20 degrees from parallel with the canoe's centerline.

2 Using torso rotation to move the blade back and forth keeps your arms in the paddler's box. Weight your offside knee to raise the side of opposition.

3 Turn your control thumb out and change the blade angle. Again, the leading edge is not more than 20 degrees from parallel with the canoe's centerline. When sculling, you are tracing a figure eight.

Solo Abeam Using Cross Sculling Draws

1 Cross sculling is similar to sculling. Rotate toward your offside. Choke up with your shaft hand to get the paddle blade aft of the pivot point. The powerface faces the hull.

2 Weight your onside knee (edge the canoe to the onside) to raise the side of opposition. Use your torso rotation to move the paddle back and forth to trace a figure eight.

3 The blade is slicing more than it is drawing water. Keep the angle of the blade no more than 20 degrees from parallel with the canoe's centerline to ensure lateral movement.

Tandem Onside Spin

There are alternative ways to spin a tandem canoe using draws, pries, sculling draws, and sculling pries. When one of these strokes is performed repeatedly in unison in the bow and stern of the tandem canoe, the canoe spins on its pivot point, though not as quickly as with sweeps. (Compare for yourself by timing three 360-degree spins with sweeps and then with draws and pries to see which is faster.) Whenever you have the opportunity to try out different canoes, observe the spinning capabilities of canoes with more or less rocker.

Just north of Bark Lake,
the shadows from giant
pine fall across our path and
our solar charging equipment shuts
off for the day. The sun's energy enabled
us to share our Ancient Forest Water Trail stories
through a sophisticated communications system.

Tandem Onside Spin Using Draws

1 *The draw stroke is demonstrated in more detail on pages 54–55. It is performed here in the same way, but the tandem canoe remains level during the spin.*

2 *Tandem canoeists performing the draw in unison cause the canoe to make an onside spin. Use torso rotation to bring your end of the canoe to the blade.*

3 *The bow paddler sets the pace. The stern paddler performs all three phases of the stroke — the catch, the draw, and the underwater slice recovery — in cadence with his partner.*

Tandem Onside Spin Using Sculling Draws

1 *Sculling draws in a tandem canoe tend to make the canoe spin more gracefully than straight draws. Concentrate on keeping your paddle shaft vertical.*

2 *Apply pressure to the blade in a continuous back-and-forth motion toward the bow and stern. The blade angle should be no more than 20 degrees off parallel with the canoe's centerline.*

3 *Torso rotation is once again the key. Keeping your arms relatively straight within the paddler's box ensures that you paddle using your torso muscles.*

Tandem Onside Abeam Using Draws and Pries

1 *Raise the side of opposition, that is, the side the canoe is moving toward. Both paddlers use upper-body rotation to stay within the paddler's box.*

2 *In unison, the bow paddler executes a draw and the stern paddler puts in a forceful pry.*

3 *The canoe is moving laterally between the buoys with neither the bow or stern leading the way. Equal force is being applied to the bow and stern.*

Tandem Onside Abeam Using Sculling Draws and Pries

1 *Sculling is much smoother than draws or pries for sideways movement. Sculling is a dynamic action that moves the canoe laterally. It is also useful at the end of a sideslip if you wish to continue the lateral movement. (See sideslips at the end of Chapter 10.)*

2 *Keep your arms relatively straight, using the rotation of your upper body to move the paddle. Your control thumb adjusts the angle on the blade. It should be slight, resulting in an action that is more like a slice, rather than pushing and pulling a lot of water.*

3 *Work in unison with your partner to ensure that the bow and stern move sideways at the same speed.*

Tandem Offside Abeam

1 Concentrate on keeping your arms relaxed but fairly straight so that it is your torso rotation that provides power to the paddle.

2 Raise the side of opposition, which, in this case, is the bow paddler's offside. In other words, edge the canoe to the bow paddler's onside.

3 Perform draw and pry strokes in unison. The bow paddler is prying and the stern paddler is drawing.

4 Both paddlers should apply equal pressure to their paddle blades to keep the canoe moving sideways smoothly.

On Lake Superior, the Earth's greatest expanse of freshwater, I can see way down into the world beneath me, to multicolored cobblestones, reefs, sand waves, bits of shipwreck, and the occasional trout. At times like these, I wish I paddled a canoe transparent as glass.

9 Moving Forward

We first encountered Lake Superior during a seven-month voyage across Canada by canoe. She welcomed us in a warm and gentle embrace. Everything about our canoe and equipment was suited for straight-ahead flatwater speed, but favorable weather was what allowed us to cover the 500-mile (800 km) north shore from Whitefish Bay to the Pigeon River in just ten days. Whether it was the day we paddled 95 miles up the north shore of Lake Winnipeg or 250 miles in three days down the Mackenzie River, paddling forward in a straight line was the technique we used ninety-nine percent of the time.

Traveling forward is what you do in a canoe most of the time, yet it is one of the most difficult things to master, whether you are heading for a destination near or far. There is more to going forward than meets the eye. We have devoted the next ten pages to examining strokes that propel you forward: the basic forward stroke and its variations — the cross forward, the J-stroke, the silent stroke, and the C-stroke. Whether you paddle on ponds, creeks, lakes, rivers, or oceans, the key ingredient for developing the skills to paddle on a desired course is endless practice on a windless waterbody.

Up to this point we have demonstrated two of the three categories of strokes: corrective strokes and righting strokes. The third category is power strokes, the ones that propel you forward.

Take a step and examine how your weight is transferred from the heel to the ball of your foot and then unweighted and transferred to the other foot. Walking is a remarkable action that we take for granted, like breathing. Although many of us could improve the efficiency of our gait, the pattern is so ingrained it is very hard to alter. When Gary and I hiked the 2,100-mile (3,360 km) Appalachian Trail, he pointed out that if I walked toes forward instead of turned out, it would take me many fewer steps to reach Maine. It didn't seem significant at the time, but when I later calculated the loss of distance per step, I discovered the cost amounted to an extra 60 miles (100 km) of unnecessary walking.

Where is all this leading? Into the forward stroke, of course. Just as our style of walking becomes ingrained, so do our paddling styles and habits. For those of you with years of canoeing experience, we hope you can adapt the techniques shown on the next few pages to complement your paddling style. We guarantee you will travel farther faster with more ease.

For those just starting out, the forward stroke presents a challenge. You may not be rewarded with the kind of instant satisfactory reponse you had with spins and abeams. That's to be expected. Avoid shortcuts, striving instead for efficient technique right from the beginning. Paddling solo or tandem, bow or stern, in headwinds or crosswinds, you will tackle them all with more confidence.

The Forward Stroke

The *forward stroke,* like all forward power strokes, takes place in front of your body, in the frontal-resistance end of the canoe. Upper body rotation, good posture, comfortably straight arms, and staying within the paddler's box are all important elements of efficient forward travel. Let's break the stroke up into steps so we can examine this most used but often improperly executed stroke.

Every paddler can appreciate the rewards of efficiency of motion. You soon realize how much easier it is to paddle into a wind and how much more energy you have when you set up camp at the end of a day's paddling.

Notice the difference in the paddler's body position between Photos 3 and 4. During the propulsion phase, you thrust your hips forward to increase speed. This forceful action of moving from a forward lean to an upright sit while you are unwinding your torso drives the canoe forward (Newton's Third Law at work again).

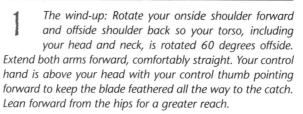

1 *The wind-up: Rotate your onside shoulder forward and offside shoulder back so your torso, including your head and neck, is rotated 60 degrees offside. Extend both arms forward, comfortably straight. Your control hand is above your head with your control thumb pointing forward to keep the blade feathered all the way to the catch. Lean forward from the hips for a greater reach.*

2 *The catch: Both hands are out over the water with your shaft hand a little ahead of your control hand. Turn your control thumb out before planting the blade perpendicular to the centerline. Keep your arms comfortably extended and drive both hands down to fully submerge the blade. The blade should slide cleanly into the water, without a big splash.*

3 *The propulsion: Power is transferred to the paddle from your upper body muscles through your arms by unwinding your torso. While keeping both arms comfortably straight, pull with your shaft arm and push with your control arm. The shaft remains vertical. Think of using your hips to thrust the canoe forward to the planted paddle.*

4 *The exit: Complete the hip thrust. Bring your shaft hand back just aft of your knee — any further and you waste energy by lifting water. Turn your control thumb forward to slice the blade cleanly from the water.*

5 *The recovery: Feather the blade all the way to the catch position. Keep both arms comfortably extended. Your control hand remains high throughout the recovery to the wind-up. (Dropping your control hand down wastes energy.)*

Shakwa Lake near the Spanish River. Drifting in the dawn mist, one can imagine a morning such as this a thousand years ago when the only sounds linking unending lakes, rivers, forests and fields were the songs of nature.

The Cross Forward Stroke

The *cross forward* is a powerful stroke that maintains forward momentum while correcting the natural tendency of the bow to veer to the offside. The cross forward brings the bow back toward the onside. This stroke is similar to the forward stroke, except it occurs on the opposite side of the canoe. The stroke uses the powerface of the blade and it takes place in front of the paddler. Upper body flexibility is important to this stroke, so keep up with your yoga.

Begin the cross forward by crossing the paddle from the onside to the offside without changing your grip on the paddle. Point your control thumb to the offside, turning the powerface of the blade up. Feather your blade cleanly across the bow without hitting the gunwales and plant the blade on your offside as close to the bow as possible. A big part of the cross foward stroke is the hip-thrust action that pulls your hips forcefully to the blade. In the cross forward, the blade comes back as far as your thigh (which means your shaft hand is just aft of your knee). Turn your control thumb forward and slice the blade straight forward in an *underwater* recovery. Be careful not to jam your blade against the bow before the catch.

1 Lean forward from the hips as you plant the paddle with the powerface toward the offside knee. Both hands are out over the water with both arms comfortably extended. Drive the control hand down to fully submerge the blade.

2 Plant the blade as close to the bow as possible. The shaft is nearly vertical with your shaft hand a bit ahead of your control hand. Bring your upper body to an upright position forcefully, pulling your hips to the blade. This is a hip thrust.

3 To avoid getting your arms tied up in knots, don't let your shaft hand go back any further than your knee. When the blade reaches your thigh, turn your control thumb forward and begin the recovery by slicing the blade straight forward to the bow for the catch.

4 An underwater recovery is efficient and smooth. The trick is to make sure the blade is sliced straight forward and not on an angle where it can jam against the bow.

1 The wind-up: Rotate your onside shoulder forward and your offside shoulder back so that your torso, including your head and neck, is rotated 60 degrees to the offside. (It helps to look in that direction.) Your control hand is above your head and your control thumb points forward.

2 The catch: Keep both arms comfortably extended, not locked. Lean forward from your hips. Just before planting the blade, turn your control thumb out to plant the blade perpendicular to the centerline. Keep your arms extended and drive the blade down to fully submerge it.

3 The propulsion: Keeping your arms comfortably straight, push forward with your control hand and pull with your shaft hand. Your torso rotates forward and past the centerline to face toward the onside. Think of your offside shoulder as a door hinge; your torso is the door swinging on this hinge.

The J-Stroke

The *J-stroke* is an onside combination stroke that provides forward momentum while keeping the canoe on a straight course. Combining these two functions smoothly is what makes the J-stroke one of the most difficult strokes to learn. It begins with an efficient forward stroke. That stroke is followed by the J, a quick course-correcting action. The J is a hook at the end of the propulsion phase. It is used to offset the turning force to the offside that is created by the forward stroke.

The J is essentially a kind of pry, but one that uses the powerface and not the backface. Many canoeists develop the unfortunate habit of converting a forward stroke into a shallow-water pry, which uses the backface of the blade. You will know you are doing this if your control thumb is pointing back instead of forward. The shallow-water pry has its place in whitewater playboating (see page 194 in Chapter 20,

Dancing with the River), but when used as a method to keep the canoe on course, it stalls forward momentum.

The J we are demonstrating here uses the powerface of the blade. When the blade reaches your hip and your shaft hand is just aft of your knee, turn your control thumb forward to initiate the J. Allow the shaft to rotate freely in your shaft hand. Keep your control hand high over the onside gunwale and in front of your body. As you pull the grip toward the offside gunwale with your control hand, you are maintaining continuous resistance against the powerface. Either the gunwale or your shaft hand has to act as a fulcrum point against which you apply the force. Keep a relaxed grip on the shaft to ensure that you don't cock your onside wrist or lift your onside elbow at this point. By the time the grip is over the centerline, the blade is in its feathered recovery position.

4 *The J: Bring the blade to your hip, then initiate the J by turning your control thumb forward. The powerface turns out. Relax your grip on the shaft. The force against the powerface remains constant as you keep your control hand high and in front of you. Pull this hand toward the offside gunwale. Here, the modern J uses the onside gunwale as a fulcrum point. Feel the resistance against the powerface of the blade. For the traditional J, hold the shaft away from the gunwale. The force of the water will be transferred to your onside arm joints (wrist, elbow, and shoulder) instead of the gunwale.*

5 *The recovery: As soon as you have finished pulling the grip toward the centerline, feather the blade in a partial underwater recovery toward the bow. Depending on how much you need to turn the bow to the onside, you can continue applying resistance to the powerface throughout the recovery. It takes many miles of canoeing to perfect the smooth transition from one phase to another in this beautiful stroke.*

Traditional paddlers prefer to keep the paddle shaft from touching the gunwale. This approach certainly has its merits. A quiet evening paddle is something less than quiet with a canoeist banging J-strokes off the gunwale, especially in an aluminum canoe. On the other hand, the modern J-stroke, which uses the gunwale for leverage, has its advantages too. Gunwales are cheaper and easier to replace than your joints. At times, when you need a quick burst of speed or you are paddling into a headwind, perhaps with a heavy load, consider trying the modern J. The gunwale provides the fulcrum point, reducing the push and pull required by your body. The practiced-to-perfection J-stroke results in a quick, smooth action that happens close to the canoe. Even if you use the gunwale during the J-stroke, you need not make a lot of noise. Follow through with a feathered recovery all the way to the catch position, keeping your arms relatively straight and your control hand high.

The Silent Stroke

The *silent stroke* is a wonderful variation on the J-stroke that, once mastered, allows you quick, quiet passage through the water. The key to the silent stroke is the recovery. Following the J, the blade is sliced back to the catch position in an underwater recovery. Roll the grip in the palm of your hand so that the backface now becomes the powerface. From stroke to stroke, the blade does not leave the water at all.

The beauty of the silent stroke is just that — the silence. You can paddle along a stretch of shoreline at dusk with the only sound of your passing being the small rippling wake slapping the rocks. A beaver swims across your path, carving its own silver V in the dark waters. Every sound of the forest is crystal clear: a creek burbling, the distant hooting of an owl, a frog croaking. Gary and I love to get out the solo canoes on a warm summer evening and explore Rabbit Lake's little bays and inlets. We know where the loons nest and where the beavers build their lodges, and occasionally we'll see a mink, an otter, or a moose. Traveling in silence takes practice but the rewards are well worth the effort.

1 The silent stroke is a forward stroke with an underwater recovery where the powerface alternates on each stroke. In this photo, the paddler is in the corrective phase of the J-stroke, using the dark backface of the paddle as the powerface.

2 Move from one blade face to the other by rolling the grip in the palm of your control hand while the blade is in the recovery position. Slice the blade forward in a complete underwater recovery. As the blade slices back to the catch, the blade's leading edge turns toward the hull instead of away from it as in a forward stroke.

3 Open your fingers on your control hand to spin the paddle grip in your palm. Now your control thumb points out. The leading edge of the blade turns toward the hull. What was the powerface now becomes the backface.

4   This is the propulsion phase of your forward stroke. Begin with a slight forward lean at the catch, with your upper body rotated toward the offside. Pull your lower body to the blade by sitting up and unwinding your torso. Again, this is the hip thrust.

5   At the end of the propulsion phase, turn your control thumb forward to initiate the J. Note that the powerface is the light side of the blade whereas in Photo 1, it was the dark side.

6   The smooth transitions between powerfaces and the silence of the stroke comes from the fact that the blade never completely breaks the surface of the water. The silent stroke involves very subtle blade control.

The C-Stroke

The *C-stroke* is a good flatwater start-up stroke to use to get a solo canoe moving forward in a straight line from a standstill. The path of the paddle resembles the letter C or an inverted C. Begin the stroke a few feet out in front of your body, as with the forward stroke, but place the blade a short distance out from the hull. Angle the blade toward the hull. Start this combination stroke with a *bow draw* (the bow comes to the blade), then move through the forward propulsion phase of the forward stroke, and end with a J in the eddy-resistance end of the canoe. This completes the C.

The stronger the C is carved, the more the canoe can be turned toward the onside. This turning force can be increased by getting your control hand out over the water, which forces the blade under the canoe, closer to the centerline. The C-stroke combination of bow draw and J-stroke can be useful when a lot of course correction is necessary. This stroke requires subtle blade control and takes a lot of practice to perfect.

1 *Rotate your upper body to the offside. Plant the blade further away from the hull than for the forward stroke. The powerface is angled toward the hull. Your control thumb is turned back.*

2 *Draw the bow of the canoe to the blade, scribing the top hook of the C. Your control thumb is pointing back and your control hand is out over the water to get the blade as close to the centerline as possible.*

3 *With your control hand out over the water, arc the blade under the canoe, through the propulsion phase of the C-stroke.*

Across the lake from our campsite on Scarecrow Lake, these pine catch the first light. Packing cameras and a lunch, we head for the trailhead where we plan to spend the day hiking to the top of Ishpatina Ridge, Ontario's highest point of land.

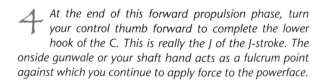

4   *At the end of this forward propulsion phase, turn your control thumb forward to complete the lower hook of the C. This is really the J of the J-stroke. The onside gunwale or your shaft hand acts as a fulcrum point against which you continue to apply force to the powerface.*

5   *Make a feathered recovery as you wind up your torso for another stroke. Depending on what will best hold you on your desired line of travel, you may follow up with a forward stroke, another C-stroke, or a J-stroke.*

In mid- to late May, when the water level is just right on Pukaskwa National Park's namesake river, we make our way down the drops in Ringham's Gorge, portaging only where necessary, around waterfalls.

Steep Rock, Lake Superior. Whether you travel alone or in the company of friends, whether you paddle solo or tandem canoes, every approach to a journey by canoe has its rewards.

10 U-Turns and Sideslips

There are a variety of ways to make U-turns in both solo and tandem canoes. They are, as the U describes, 180-degree changes in direction while on the move. Whitewater paddlers will find it worthwhile to practice U-turns on flatwater, as the exercise mimics eddy turns and peel-outs and working with river obstacles. It is helpful to have a fixed point, like our buoy, around which to turn. Three things to keep in mind while doing U-turns: you need speed, the canoe needs to be edging into the turn, and it needs to be angled in the direction of the turn. Let's start with solo U-turns. The Duffek is the stroke of choice for making onside U-turns.

Solo Onside U-Turn Using a Duffek

Next time you are running down a trail in the forest, look out for a strong young tree with a little space around it. With your palms out and thumbs pointed toward each other, grab the trunk and fling yourself around it to face in the opposite direction. That's the feeling of a U-turn done with a *Duffek*.

This stroke, named after the Czechoslovakian paddler who first used it in competition, is a *turning high brace* or *hanging draw* useful for converting forward speed into a quick turn. The Duffek is a *static* stroke. That means you need water resistance against the blade, which is created on flatwater by forward momentum and on a river by the current. (Up to this point, all the strokes demonstrated have been *dynamic,* meaning the blade position changes during the propulsion.)

Practice the Duffek position before you actually make the U-turn. Rotate your upper body about 45 degrees toward your onside gunwale. Plant the paddle with the blade opposite your knee and the powerface aimed toward the bow. The paddle shaft is nearly vertical and both hands are over the water. The direction of the force against the blade can pull the blade back, causing injury. To protect your onside shoulder from injury, keep your arms bent. Keep your onside arm tucked in close enough that you could hold an apple in your armpit. Your control arm is bent with the elbow down, and the back of your control hand is near your forehead.

Once you have practiced the position, get up some forward speed heading toward your target. Approach on an angle and begin edging the canoe *before* anchoring the Duffek. (You and the canoe will swing in an onside turn around the paddle, just like swinging around the tree.) Once you have turned, rotate your onside shoulder forward, bringing the bow to the blade. Lean forward from the hips and conclude with a forward stroke, maintaining consistent pressure on the blade throughout the maneuver.

1 *Heading toward your target, get up some forward speed. Initiate the onside turn by edging into the turn, weighting your onside knee. Angle the bow in the direction of the turn.*

2 *Rotate your upper body 45 degrees to your onside gunwale. Raise your control hand for a high shaft-angle and anchor your paddle opposite your knee. Aim the powerface toward the bow.*

3 *Make sure both hands are out over the water. Your control hand is in front of your forehead. Keep both arms tucked in fairly close to your body to prevent the risk of shoulder injury.*

4 *The Duffek is a static stroke around which the canoe turns. Your control thumb is facing back during the Duffek.*

5 *Rotate your onside shoulder forward. Once the bow reaches the blade, make a smooth transition into a forward stroke.*

6 *Keep a consistent pressure on the blade from the time you plant the Duffek through to the forward stroke. Unwind your upper body and propel the canoe forward, completing the U-turn.*

Solo Onside U-Turn Using a Compound Reverse Sweep

The reverse sweeping low brace (not shown) and the compound reverse sweep (shown) are other ways in which you can do an onside U-turn. They are important alternatives for turning in whitewater when the eddies are shallow or small, and for when you must slow forward momentum when coming into a turn.

The *reverse sweeping low brace* is similar to the reverse sweep (see the onside spin on pages 46–47) except that the paddler edges into the turn throughout the entire stroke. Rotate your torso toward the onside gunwale. Reach both hands out over the water, holding the paddle with a low shaft-angle. The powerface is turned up. The leading edge of the blade is on a climbing angle. The reverse sweeping low brace is actually a bracing force that stops forward momentum, causing the canoe to make a crisp and immediate change of direction. The extreme edging creates more rocker, which helps to spin the canoe. The edging also sinks the hull deeper in the water, providing more surface resistance. This halts the canoe's forward momentum much faster than a Duffek would. When the bow reaches the blade, make a smooth transition into a forward stroke.

A *compound reverse sweep* is demonstrated here. It begins with the reverse sweeping low brace and concludes with a Duffek. As the word "compound" implies, the blade face changes during the propulsion phase. When the blade is halfway through the sweep, raise your control hand from a low shaft-angle to a high shaft-angle. Point your control thumb toward your onside armpit, putting the blade in the Duffek position. In the first half of the maneuver, the reverse sweeping low brace is used to keep a consistent pressure on the backface of the blade; then, during the Duffek phase, a consistent pressure is on the powerface of the blade. Once the bow swings to the blade at the completion of the Duffek, make a smooth transition into a forward stroke.

1 Approach the turn with forward momentum. Angle the canoe in the direction of the turn. Edge the canoe to the onside.

2 Rotate your upper body to face the onside gunwale. Keep the shaft angle low with both hands over the water. Keep the blade on a climbing angle.

3 Unwind your torso, bringing your onside shoulder forward until the paddle blade is opposite your hip.

4 Raise your control hand so the paddle has a high shaft-angle. Your control thumb goes from pointing forward to pointing at your onside shoulder. This flips the blade into the Duffek position, which uses the powerface of the blade.

5 Continue rotating your upper body forward, bringing the bow to the blade. Once the bow meets the blade, make a smooth transition into a forward stroke.

Solo Offside U-Turn Using the Cross Duffek

Don a scuba mask and dive beneath the surface at the marker buoy to get a fresh perspective of the canoe, canoeist, and paddle. Look up toward the surface. From a fish's viewpoint, there is no difference between a U-turn done with a cross Duffek and one done with a Duffek. For the paddler, the cross Duffek is merely the offside version of the Duffek.

Establish the angle of the canoe and begin edging before you plant the cross Duffek to make the turn. Once again, speed is necessary to create the water resistance against which the blade braces. Rotate your upper body to face the offside gunwale, and anchor the blade beside your offside knee with the powerface toward the bow. Both hands are over the water. Bring the bow to the blade by unwinding your torso. Then follow up with a strong cross forward stroke. Thrust your lower body forcefully forward, bringing your hips to the blade.

1 Approach the turn with momentum. Initiate the offside U-turn with a forward sweep to get the canoe turning in the direction you want it to go. Weight your offside knee so that you are edging into the turn. Feather the blade over the bow parallel to the deck.

2 Plant the cross Duffek beside your offside knee at a 45-degree angle, with the powerface toward the bow. Keep both hands over the water.

3 Unwind your torso, bringing your onside shoulder back. The bow comes to the blade. Hold the paddle in the cross Duffek, a static, high-angle position in front of your body. Your control thumb points forward, and both arms are bent with elbows down. Keep edging to the offside.

4 When the bow meets the blade, turn your control thumb so that the blade faces your offside knee. Both hands remain over the water.

5 Make a smooth transition from the cross Duffek into a strong cross forward stroke. Conclude by bringing your blade back to your onside. Take a forward stroke.

Solo Offside U-Turn Using Sliding Pry and Slice

The solo offside U-turn using a sliding pry and slice is a very exciting offside turn that uses a more advanced technique of edging to the outside of the turn. Part of what makes this maneuver more difficult than the other U-turns is the fact that by edging to the outside with your paddle in close to the hull, you are depending on good boat control with your body weight balanced. Maintaining an upright upper body is essential or you will end up swimming.

Once again, initiate the turn with a forward sweep that will get you turning to the offside. Following the forward sweep, knife the blade toward the hull with a high shaft-angle as if you are setting up for a pry. Turn your control thumb back. Slide the vertical shaft forward along the gunwale. Rotate your onside shoulder forward. The blade's leading edge is against the hull. The force of the water is against the backface of the paddle.

This is the *sliding pry* and, like any pry, it forces the canoe away from the paddle or, more specifically in this case, the bow moves toward the offside, away from the paddle. Sliding the pry forward along the gunwale is once again the work of your torso muscles. You are actually winding your upper body into the same position as you would for the catch in the forward stroke.

When the blade is as far forward as you can comfortably reach, quickly turn your control thumb forward so the powerface is now angled away from the hull on a 45-degree angle. This begins the *slice*. It looks similar to the forward stroke, but the canoe responds differently. The inside edge of the blade is leading the pull back as the shaft slides along the gunwale. The action continues to force the bow away from the blade as in a pry. When done well, this elegant combination of the sliding pry and the slice causes one continuous movement of the bow to the offside.

1 *Initiate the offside turn with a forward sweep. Keep your weight on your onside knee. You are edging to the outside of the turn.*

2 Following the sweep stroke, lift your control hand with the control thumb pointing out. Knife the leading edge of the blade to meet the hull as if you are setting up a pry. Turn your control thumb back.

3 The paddle shaft is vertical and the blade is angled with the leading edge of the blade closest to the hull. The force of the water is on the backface of the blade. This is the beginning of the sliding pry.

4 Rotate your onside shoulder forward as you slide the shaft along the gunwale toward the bow. The force of the water is still on the backface of the blade. Your J-lean is critical for maintaining your balance.

5 Rotate your torso all the way to your offside as in the wind-up for the forward stroke. Reach as far forward as you can with your onside arm. Then turn your control thumb forward to set the new angle of the blade for the slice.

6 The slice is performed the same way as a forward stroke except the blade angle is at 45 degrees instead of 90 degrees to the centerline. The inside edge is leading the pull back.

7 The slice continues to force the bow to the offside. By aggressively pulling your hips to the blade while unwinding your torso and sitting upright, you are using the hip thrust to propel you forward.

Tandem Onside U-Turns

In a *tandem U-turn*, as a general rule, if the canoe is turning toward your paddling side, you are responsible for setting the edge. The other paddler helps to hold this edge. Speed, edge, and angle are the key features to any U-turn, whether solo or tandem.

In these two sequences, shown on pages 87 and 89, the bow paddler is responsible for setting the edge for the *onside U-turn*. The stern paddler helps to maintain it. In the first sequence the bow paddler uses a Duffek and in the second sequence, a compound reverse sweep. For this onside turn, the Duffek is the better choice for maintaining speed throughout the turn. However, there are circumstances when you will need to arrest your forward momentum and turn the canoe on a dime, and this is when the reverse sweeping low brace and compound reverse sweep are very useful.

Tandem Onside U-Turn Using a Duffek

1   Approach with momentum and angle the canoe in the direction of the turn. Edge the canoe to the onside. The bow paddler plants a Duffek while the stern paddler initiates a series of quarter forward sweeps (stern sweeps).

2   The Duffek is the anchor point around which the canoe turns. The bow paddler protects his onside shoulder from injury by keeping his elbows bent and tucked in to his sides.

3   The stern paddler continues doing stern sweeps while holding the onside edge throughout. Both paddlers keep their bodies within the paddler's box.

4   Once the bow reaches the blade, the bow paddler makes a smooth transition into a forward stroke. At the same time, the stern paddler feathers her blade back to the catch for a forward stroke.

5   Reach forward with good shoulder rotation. Plant your blades and take forward strokes in unison for smooth forward momentum.

Denison Falls is the thundering finale to a journey down the Dog River, which ends in Lake Superior just west of Michipicoten Harbour.

Tandem Onside U-Turn Using a Compound Reverse Sweep

1 *Approach the turn with speed. Edge the canoe to the onside in the direction of the turn.*

4 *When the bow paddler uses the reverse sweeping low brace, the stern paddler's stern sweeps help keep the canoe spinning.*

2 *The bow paddler unwinds his torso, bringing the onside shoulder forward with the reverse sweeping low brace. Both paddlers continue to hold the edge while the stern paddler assists with stern sweeps.*

3 *The canoe spins, but forward momentum stalls (which is the effect you want). The bow paddler completes the U-turn by flipping the blade to the powerface and into a Duffek.*

5 *Once the U-turn is complete, both paddlers follow up with forward strokes. The U-turn is dependent on your approach speed, the hull shape, and how much the canoe is edged through the turn.*

Tandem Offside U-Turn Using a Cross Duffek

1 *Angle and edge the canoe into the offside turn. Initiate this U-turn with a forward quarter sweep in the bow and a reverse sweeping low brace in the stern.*

2 *Plant a cross Duffek in the bow. The stern paddler's hands are low and over the water. Notice the body rotation of both paddlers. The stern paddler sets the edge and both paddlers hold it.*

3 *Continue to hold the edge as the canoe begins to turn. The bow paddler is weighting his offside knee and the stern paddler is weighting her onside knee.*

Tandem Offside U-Turn Using a Sliding Pry and Slice

1 *Approach the turn with lots of speed. The stern paddler initiates the offside U-turn with a reverse sweeping low brace while at the same time edging to the offside, contrary to the rule of edging into the turn.*

2 *The bow paddler slices the blade into the hull. You will find that the blade is pinned against the hull until the canoe loses some of its momentum.*

3 *Both paddlers continue edging the canoe to the outside of the turn. Your J-lean is crucial for maintaining balance. This is a fast and thrilling U-turn.*

4 The stern paddler rotates forward with the reverse sweeping low brace, kicking the stern to the offside, while the bow paddler brings the bow to the blade with the cross Duffek.

5 Both paddlers reach forward to follow through with power strokes; the stern paddler with a forward stroke and the bow paddler with a cross forward.

6 The bow paddler returns his blade to the onside, and both paddlers reach forward with good shoulder rotation to complete the maneuver with forward strokes in unison.

4 As the bow paddler feels the turning momentum decreasing, he begins sliding the pry forward along the gunwale. The stern paddler rotates forward with the reverse sweeping low brace.

5 In the bow, bring the paddle as far forward as possible with the sliding pry. In the stern, raise your control hand for a high shaft-angle. Both paddlers prepare for a forward slice.

6 Slice strokes are similar to forward strokes except the powerface is angled out at 45 degrees instead of 90 degrees to the centerline. When you apply force, the canoe moves forward and away.

Sideslips

On flatwater and in river running, *sideslipping* is a useful maneuver that allows you to avoid obstacles without having to turn, change direction, or sacrifice speed. It is simple and easy to learn, yet many canoeists never use it. Here are a couple of instances where you might want to sideslip. You are paddling along a lakeshore when you notice a stump barely protruding above the surface. With no time to stop or change direction, you can avoid the obstacle with a quick sideslip and carry on as if nothing is amiss. Or suppose you're paddling a river in a heavily loaded tandem canoe. A falcon dives across the cliff, drawing your attention away from your path. Suddenly a rock looms dead ahead. A turn will broadside the canoe for sure, but a simple sideslip will enable you to avoid the obstacle and carry on downriver.

Instead of real rocks and stumps, we are back to our colored buoys. Our aim is to shift or sideslip the canoe laterally between the buoys without allowing the canoe to spin forward or backward. Refer back to the draw, pry, and sculling strokes in Chapter 8 on pages 54–59. These strokes were used in their *dynamic* form for abeams. Remember the dynamic shoulder rotation required to draw the canoe to the blade, and the dynamic pry required to push the canoe away from the blade. Sideslips instead use the *static* forms of these strokes.

The sideslip maneuver shown on the next few pages requires forward momentum in order to create a force against the static blade position. Just place a static stroke in the water and let the water act against it. Think less of the stroke and more about the blade angle. The single most important thing to remember with sideslips is that *the blade angle points in the direction you want to go.* It doesn't matter if you do them solo or tandem, forward or backward, this rule holds true. While sideslipping, it is important as always to raise your side of opposition to reduce the resistance against the hull as you move laterally across the water. If you need to continue moving sideways after the canoe has lost momentum with the sideslip, then you convert your stationary stroke into its dynamic form.

Solo Onside Sideslip Using a Stationary Draw

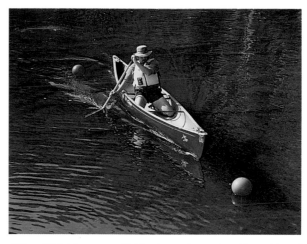

1 It is important to have straight-ahead speed before initiating the sideslip. In order to see what the sideslip is doing, we set up the two marker buoys a little more than one canoe-length apart. Practicing with such a setup helps you to develop finesse and accuracy with sideslips.

2 On passing the first buoy, the paddler positions the blade in a stationary draw with the blade angled. This resembles the Duffek except the blade is set slightly behind the paddler. Keep the shaft angle high throughout.

3 Weight your offside knee to raise the side of opposition. This increases the efficiency of your onside sideways movement. (In a whitewater canoe outfitted with thigh straps, the onside knee can assist this effort by lifting the onside gunwale.)

4 The powerface is aimed toward your body instead of the bow. The blade angle is about 15 to 20 degrees from parallel to the centerline, with the leading edge of the blade further from the hull than the following edge.

5 When you have moved far enough over to avoid the obstacle, slice the blade forward into a forward stroke.

The Wanapitei originates from a long, thin ribbon of water
called Scotia Lake. On one of the lake's rock walls
we discovered pictographs painted with
red ochre by paddlers of long ago.

Solo Offside Sideslip Using a Stationary Cross Draw

1 It is important to have straight-ahead speed to effectively sideslip the canoe.

2 Use the stationary cross draw to move the canoe laterally to the offside. *This stroke is similar to the cross Duffek, except the blade is anchored slightly behind your body.*

3 Raise the side of opposition by weighting your onside knee. *This action increases the efficiency of the lateral movement to your offside.*

4 Choke up with your shaft hand. Your control hand remains in front of your body. *The powerface is facing your body and not the bow as it would be in a cross Duffek. Keep a high shaft-angle throughout.*

5 Once you have sideslipped as far as you want, bring the blade back to your onside and take a forward stroke.

1 *Get up some straight-ahead speed before initiating the sideslip. This offside sideslip uses a stationary (static) pry to move the canoe laterally to the offside.*

2   *At the end of the forward stroke, turn your control thumb back and slice the blade into the hull with the backface out. The blade is at your thigh, held stationary with the powerface aimed toward you. The paddle shaft is vertical.*

3   *Weight your onside knee to raise the side of opposition so the canoe will move with greater ease to the offside.*

4   *This maneuver is good practice for keeping your weight balanced over the centerline. If you lean over the gunwale instead of keeping your body in the J-lean position, you will likely tip.*

5   *Keep the paddle in a static pry position until you have moved sideways to the offside as far as you want. If the canoe has lost momentum and you want to continue moving laterally, turn the static pry into a dynamic pry (see pages 56–57) as demonstrated.*

Tandem Sideslips

A sideslip is an elegant way to shift the canoe sideways while underway. It is an efficient way for both solo and tandem canoes to avoid obstacles while maintaining forward speed without turning the canoe. Sideslips are especially useful to tandem canoes on moving water, and we hope that these demonstrations encourage you to use them often. Forward speed is required with all sideslips because the force that moves the canoe is created by the movement of water against the paddle blade rather than the paddle blade against the water.

The same strokes are used — a combination of the static pry and the static draw — for the tandem onside and offside sideslips. For an offside sideslip, the bow paddler uses a static pry and the stern paddler, a static draw. For an onside sideslip it is reversed. The paddler in the frontal-resistance end of the canoe has to keep the angle of his blade in check. If opened up too wide, that end of the canoe sideslips faster than the eddy-resistance or following end. Raise the side of opposition to enhance the lateral movement. When the momentum slows but you still want to continue sideways movement, just turn the static strokes into dynamic ones. Sculling strokes are useful here. See Chapter 8, pages 58–59.

The most important thing to concentrate on is the direction in which you wish the canoe to go. *Aim the leading edge of your blade in that direction.*

Tandem Onside Sideslips

1 — *Approach with forward momentum. The more speed you have, the more force against the blade, the further you can sideslip.*

2 — *Raise the side of opposition. The bow paddler places a static draw while the stern paddler places a static pry. Both blades are angled 15 to 20 degrees from parallel with the centerline. Aim the leading edge of the blade where you want to go.*

Tandem Offside Sideslips

1 — *It is fun to practice sideslipping anytime you are paddling straight ahead.*

2 — *Raise the side of opposition and J-lean your body. The stern paddler places a static draw.*

3 *The bow paddler can increase her blade angle a little more if the canoe needs to be shifted sideways faster. It may slow forward momentum but it is better than hitting the obstacle.*

4 *The stern paddler keeps the stern aligned with the bow by adjusting his blade angle. The bow paddler has to be aware that her sideslipping speed may be faster than the stern's movement with the static pry.*

5 *If you want to continue moving abeam when the sideslip's momentum has slowed, turn the static strokes into dynamic ones. Here, the stern paddler does pries in unison with the bow paddler's draws.*

3 *Simultaneously, the bow paddler places a static pry. The bow paddler has to adjust the angle of her blade so the bow does not sideslip faster than the stern.*

4 *The stern paddler adjusts his blade angle to maintain the straight-ahead alignment of the canoe.*

5 *Once the canoe loses momentum, both paddlers can keep the lateral movement going by turning their static strokes into dynamic ones. Follow through with forward strokes.*

11 Moving Backward

Learning to paddle backward makes you a more well-rounded and versatile paddler. Everything we have demonstrated so far can be practiced in reverse, though some of the strokes require a lot more flexibility. Paddling in reverse requires less analytical thinking about specific strokes and more of a feel for the direction in which you wish to go.

When you move in reverse, the words "stern" and "bow" become, like "left" and "right," confusing. Let's instead go back to the Fundamentals of Paddling in Chapter 4 and think of the canoe in terms of the leading, or frontal-resistance, end and the following, or eddy-resistance, end. It helps to keep in mind that when the canoe has a symmetrically shaped hull, as all of ours do, it makes no difference to the water whether the canoe is carving a path bow-first or stern-first. In other words, you need only remember that power and control strokes take place in the frontal-resistance end of the canoe, and turning and corrective strokes take place in the eddy-resistance end of the canoe.

This knowledge is especially helpful while paddling tandem in reverse. If both paddlers are comfortable with bow and stern responsibilities, then the reversal of roles that happens when paddling backward is not a big deal. Up to now you have increased your repertoire of strokes by learning them on both sides and by paddling bow and stern. Learning to do everything in reverse simply adds to the fun and challenge of flatwater canoeing. If you are planning to progress to moving water, we assure you that mastering the art of paddling backward will be well worth your effort. Paddling backward is an essential skill for ferries, sideslips, eddy turns, and peel-outs, and for halting forward travel.

1 The catch: Rotate your onside shoulder toward the stern. Place the blade 18 inches (45 cm) behind you. Your control thumb is turned out and you are exerting force on the blade's backface. Lean back from the hips.

2 The propulsion: Rotate your onside shoulder forward. Both arms are comfortably bent. Push with your shaft hand and pull with your control hand.

3 Bring the shaft to a vertical position quickly, maintaining the position through to the completion of the propulsion phase. The blade remains at right angles to the centerline throughout the stroke.

The Back Stroke

Begin the *back stroke* by rotating toward your onside gunwale. You will be applying force to the backside of the blade throughout the stroke. Turn your control thumb out to get the blade angle correct. Lean back from your hips at the catch. Place the blade in the water 18 inches (45 cm) behind your body. Pull with your control hand while pushing with your shaft hand, quickly bringing the paddle shaft to a vertical position. Maintain this high shaft-angle as you rotate your torso forward. At the end of the propulsion phase, you should be leaning forward at the hips with a good reach to the bow. You will end up in the position that you would be in for the catch phase of the forward stroke. Keep the blade angled at 90 degrees to the centerline throughout the stroke. To recover, turn your control thumb back, slice the blade from the water, and feather it back in the direction of your thumb. Just before the catch, turn your control thumb out to plant the blade correctly for the next stroke.

4 *The exit: A comparison of Photos 1 and 4 shows just how much the upper body rotates on the back stroke from the catch to the exit. By the exit phase, you are leaning forward from the hips.*

5 *The recovery: Feather the blade out of the water, following the direction of your control thumb; it is pointing back. Just before the catch, turn your control thumb out and plant the blade for the next stroke.*

The Back and Cross Back Strokes

In the same way a cross forward offsets the turning effect of a forward stroke, a cross back offsets the turning effect of a back stroke. The *back* and *cross back* are used in combination by solo paddlers in river paddling to get up momentum from a dead stop while keeping the canoe on a straight course. It is also a powerful combination for back ferrying in strong currents.

1 *Rotate your onside shoulder back toward the stern. Your control thumb points out. Force will be applied to the paddle's backface.*

2 *The paddle shaft is vertical and the blade is perpendicular and as close to the centerline as possible.*

3 *Compare these first three images to the side-on views on the previous pages. Note how much you have to rotate your torso while doing the back stroke.*

4   *The cross back: Feather the blade across the bow with your control thumb leading the way. Place the blade behind your body with your control thumb out so that you are applying force to the powerface of the paddle.*

5   *You will have to lean back slightly and rotate your shoulders a great deal in order to be in the correct position. Drive the blade down with your control hand and pull with your shaft hand while unwinding your torso toward the bow.*

6   *The propulsion phase ends at your knee. For repeated cross backs, make an underwater recovery with your control thumb pointing forward. (This is an exception to the rule that the control thumb points in the direction of recovery.)*

The Compound Back Stroke

1 The catch: Rotate your upper body toward your onside. Lean back. Plant the blade with a high shaft-angle and as far back behind your body as possible. Your control thumb points toward the canoe.

2 The propulsion: You are looking at the powerface. Apply force to this blade face as you rotate your onside shoulder forward. This is the far back part of the compound back stroke.

A compound stroke is any stroke in which force is applied to one face of the paddle blade and then the other during the entire propulsion phase of the stroke. The *compound back,* which is performed on your onside, is an example of this. When it is used in conjunction with the reverse J, it is a good way to get your canoe moving in reverse in a straight line from a dead stop. The compound back is a combination of the far back and the back stroke.

Begin the *far back* by rotating your torso 90 degrees to your onside so you can place the blade in the water as far behind your body as possible. Your control thumb will be pointing toward the canoe and you will be looking at the powerface. Keeping the paddle shaft vertical, begin unwinding your torso to pull the canoe to the blade. When the blade is just behind you, turn your control thumb out and finish the propulsion phase using the backface of the blade. This is the back stroke, which we have already learned. Complete the compound back with a reverse J by turning the control thumb back at the end of the propulsion phase. Continue applying force against the backface by once again using your shaft hand or the gunwale as a fulcrum point. Remember, a J is a kind of pry executed at the end of the propulsion phase to counteract the canoe's natural tendency to veer to the offside. Feather the blade from the water, recovering to the catch position in one big arc toward the stern. Once the canoe is underway, use back strokes and reverse Js to keep the canoe on course.

3   *When the blade is just behind you, turn your control thumb away from the canoe. This flips the blade face so that you are now applying pressure to the backface.*

4   *You are now performing the back stroke part of the compound back. Your onside shoulder continues rotating forward, with your shaft hand pushing and your control hand pulling.*

5   *Bring the shaft of the paddle to an upright position quickly. Maintain the blade angle at right angles to the centerline.*

6   *Continue the back stroke through to the end of the propulsion phase. Note the degree of shoulder rotation between Photos 2 and 6.*

7   *To halt the canoe's natural tendency to turn to the offside, complete the propulsion phase with a reverse J. Turn your control thumb back. Apply pressure to the backface of the blade by using the gunwale or your shaft hand as the fulcrum point. The reverse J is most effective when you get the blade well under the canoe.*

8   *Feather the blade out of the water, recovering in the same way as you do for a back stroke, with your control thumb pointing toward the stern.*

Tandem Reverse Travel

Traveling in reverse serves many useful purposes, especially in river paddling. In a tandem canoe, the roles of forward travel are reversed. The bow paddler is now in the eddy-resistance end of the canoe and is therefore responsible for keeping the canoe on course. The stern paddler is now in the leading end of the canoe, providing power. Both paddlers rotate back and look in the direction they are headed. Plant your blade at right angles to the canoe's centerline. It is important to keep the paddle shaft vertical and close to the hull to avoid doing reverse sweeps. At the end of the propulsion phase, the bow paddler executes a reverse J. Your control hand needs to be well over the water to get the blade under the hull. Both paddlers feather their blades back to the catch position. Look over your shoulder as you reach back to the catch position. Turn your control thumb out just before you insert your blade for another stroke.

1 Both paddlers rotate toward their paddling sides and lean back. Plant the blade 18 inches (45 cm) behind you. Apply force to the backface of the blade. Push with the shaft hand and pull with the control hand. Watch where you are going.

2 Both paddlers unwind their torsos by bringing the onside shoulder toward the bow. The blade is fully submerged. Keep the blade at right angles to the centerline and the shaft close to the gunwale.

3 Keep the shaft vertical once the blade passes your hip. Your shaft arm is comfortably straight through all phases. Both paddlers rotate the onside shoulder forward.

4 At the end of the propulsion phase, the bow paddler applies force to the backface to execute the reverse J. Then he feathers the blade back to the catch position in unison with the stern paddler's recovery.

From the top of this outcropping of honeycomb-shaped volcanic rock known as columnar basalt, the view east and west is of the Rossport Islands and south, to the horizon. So vast is this expanse of freshwater that some people refer to Lake Superior as an inland sea.

Tandem Reverse U-Turn

Paddling in reverse as a tandem team is fun on flatwater and very useful in river paddling. All the U-turns and sideslips that we have shown can be done in reverse. Here's just one example of taking a forward maneuver and doing it in reverse. In river paddling, reverse ferries are used often and reverse peel-outs are challenging, but when it comes to the unplanned times when you miss an eddy and find yourself inadvertently going down the river backward, you will be glad you know how to paddle in reverse. You can nonchalantly carry on as if you were facing forward.

Learning to paddle in reverse makes you think again about the bigger concepts of canoe angle, edging into the turn, and knowing where the force of the water is being exerted on canoe and blade. If you sit on the lake bottom wearing a dive mask and watch a tandem reverse U-turn taking place overhead, you cannot tell the difference between it and a tandem onside U-turn using a Duffek. The Duffek is planted with the same blade angle; the canoe carves into the turn; and the sweeps are performed in the eddy-resistance end of the canoe. You stop thinking about bow and stern altogether and, instead, think only of the frontal-resistance end and the eddy-resistance end of the canoe. The water recognizes only a hull making a footprint in its surface. The canoe and paddle blades recognize only the force of water against them.

1 Initiate the turn with momentum and angle. This U-turn is called a reverse offside U-turn because the canoe is turning away from the bow paddler's designated paddling side.

2 Edge the canoe into the turn. The bow paddler does reverse quarter sweeps to bring the eddy-resistance end to the blade. The stern paddler plants a reverse Duffek.

3 Notice how the side of opposition is raised. The bow paddler recovers with a feathered blade, repeating the quarter sweeps. The stern paddler holds the Duffek. The powerface is turned toward the canoe's frontal-resistance end as the canoe comes to the blade.

4 Once the frontal-resistance end has turned to meet the blade, the stern paddler turns his control thumb out and performs a back stroke. The bow paddler takes a back stroke in unison with the stern paddler.

5 To get the canoe on a straight-ahead course, again following the U-turn, the bow paddler uses a reverse J at the end of her back stroke.

12 Flatwater Rescues

On many of our long-distance journeys, Gary and I are away for long periods of time paddling either in solo canoes or a tandem canoe, just the two of us. Whether you are traveling with companions or alone, you have the personal responsibility to rescue yourself rather than relying upon others to do so.

If there are just two of you in one tandem canoe, a capsize means self-rescue. Although not necessary, learning to be a strong swimmer adds a definite plus to your repertoire of skills as a canoeist: feeling competent *in* the water, you feel more assured *on* the water. If you are close to shore, you can swim with your swamped canoe. If you are far away from shore, you will need to get as much of the water out as possible and attempt to reenter it. If the canoe is upside down, the first thing you have to do is turn it upright. To get some of the water out, shove the canoe back and forth from the ends or rock it side to side, sloshing as much water out over the gunwales as possible. To get back into the partially swamped canoe from the water, grab the near gunwale then reach across to the far gunwale with the other hand. Pull yourself across the near gunwale, twist, and land, backside first, into the canoe. With two people, it is easier to stabilize the canoe as you get in. Bail the remaining water out or paddle it to shore.

Tandem Self-Rescue: The Capistrano Flip

Another deep-water self-rescue, one that is faster and easier given the lightweight Kevlar canoes of today, is the *Capistrano Flip.* This method is illustrated here. Practicing step by step in controlled conditions is very helpful for the time when you need it most. Capsizes often occur in rough and windy conditions. The first thing to do with the Capistrano Flip is loop one painter around your wrist so the canoe won't take off in the wind once righted. (This is a flatwater technique only, as you would never tie a canoe to yourself in moving water.) If you synchronize your scissor kicks and throw the canoe up and over at just the right moment, you can get the canoe floating upright without too much water aboard. It's an addition to your bag of tricks to get you out of a difficult situation. It is also a fun exercise in coordination between tandem paddling partners.

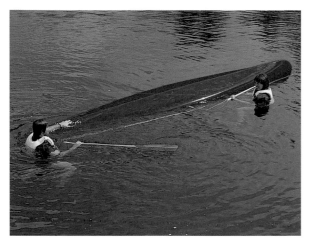

1 *Both paddlers get to the same side of the capsized canoe still holding their paddles. One paddler makes a loop in the painter and puts it around his wrist to prevent the canoe from getting carried away by the wind. Lift the gunwale nearest you up out of the water.*

2 *Face each other and tuck your paddles safely between the thwarts and seats so they won't float away. In unison, on a count of three, tip the canoe back over you.*

3 *Use the momentum of this action, along with a strong scissor kick while straightening your arms to push the canoe up and over to one side. The idea is to roll it upright in the air.*

4 *Although you may not get all the water out, there will be enough freeboard to allow you to reenter the canoe, bail it out, and paddle to shore.*

5 *Reposition yourselves on opposite sides and at opposite ends of the canoe. If your teamwork is good enough you can both get in the canoe at the same time. Hold the gunwale and together give a strong scissor kick to get yourselves out of the water.*

6 *Time your actions to coincide with your partner's effort. Lean forward, keeping your torso weight as close to the centerline as possible. Reach across to the opposite gunwale, twist, and flop your backside into the canoe.*

Canoe-over-Canoe Rescue

1 *The rescuer positions himself perpendicular to the capsized canoe. To assist the rescuer, the rescuee (swimmer) holds on to her paddle and canoe. This is especially important in a strong wind.*

2 *If you are the swimmer, put your paddle in your rescuer's canoe and then swim to the bow, where you can help stabilize the rescue canoe.*

3 *The overturned canoe is full of water and very heavy. Once the rescuer has lifted one end to break the airlock between the canoe and the water surface, the canoe is immediately lighter to lift.*

To the Rescue

Early on in our life together, Gary was forever coming to my rescue. During a winter ski trip when I accidentally plunged into the frigid black waters of a deep flowing river, Gary reacted swiftly to retrieve me by grabbing my hair as I was about to disappear under the ice and be swept away by the current. He pulled me back up the riverbank. Evening was upon us and it was nearing 40 below. Gary threw snow on me to soak up the moisture. Despite a fast ski back to camp, my clothes had frozen stiff. I was no worse for wear but a lot wiser. I was lucky.

On another occasion during an early spring canoe trip on Georgian Bay, I capsized while playing around a floating chunk of ice. I soon realized how very little time one can survive in cold water. Gary was there once again. In seconds, he had grabbed my overturned canoe, slid it across the gunwales of his canoe, emptied the water, flipped my canoe upright and slid it back into the water so that I could hoist myself aboard. Even though I was able to change my clothes quickly, my lips were blue and I was shaking for hours afterward. I remember being grateful that I was wearing my lifejacket to provide buoyancy, and for the fact that we had spent time working on our canoe-over-canoe rescue.

There isn't time for deliberation in such unpremeditated capsizes. A patterned, practiced, and speedy response on both the parts of res-

cuer and rescuee is based on the understanding that getting the swimmer out of cold water as fast as possible is of paramount importance.

In such cold water, seconds count (see hypothermia in Chapter 2). I was losing body heat at an incredible rate. In warm water, I could have swum the distance to shore in a few minutes. But in with the ice, I probably wouldn't have made it at all. Had Gary been a distance away, my best bet would have been to drape myself across the overturned hull to get as much of my body out of the water to conserve body heat until he reached me.

4 As the rescuer slides the canoe across the gunwales, the water drains out. This position is stable on calm water, but in a rolling sea you need to work quickly.

5 The rescuer now rolls the canoe away from himself by lifting the nearest gunwale on the overturned canoe. Upright and empty, the canoe slides quickly back into the water.

6 The rescuer swings the canoe around so that the canoes are parallel. If you are the swimmer, move quickly, hand over hand, along the now-uprighted canoe to a point amidships.

7 If the design of the gunwales on the two canoes permits, the rescuer can squeeze them together with his gunwale on top. In rolling waves, this secure grip helps the rescuer counterbalance the weight of the reentering paddler.

8 Using a scissor kick, the swimmer hoists herself up, and with a hand on each gunwale, twists to face forward and flops into the canoe. If the swimmer has trouble hoisting herself up, the gunwale on the swimmer's side can be lowered toward the water.

9 The rescuer holds the canoe, balancing it until the rescued canoeist has assumed the kneeling ready position. Once both canoeists have paddle in hand, they are on their way again. Under controlled conditions, this procedure should take no more than 30 seconds.

Gary and I enjoyed some of our first whitewater canoeing together on the Gull River in Minden, Ontario. The river has since been designated the Minden Wildwater Preserve, and international whitewater championships are held here.

13 Moving Water

Rivers are the flowing journeys that have always defined the landscape we call home. Thousands of them weave together a vast network of lakes across Ontario. They meander through the valleys where we played as children. Their crooked courses tumble in and out of northern lakes, whispering to us of summer's adventures: "Follow me, follow me." When we paddled across Canada, Gary and I were in pursuit of a dream, a dream to link oceans by crossing a continent via its waterways.

Rivers great and small characterize communities and distinguish those who live along them. They are wonderful corridors for wildlife. Birds follow them during their migrations south and north. In places where the rivers flow clean and pure, we've enjoyed many a fish dinner of fresh brook trout or arctic grayling. We have paddled in the St. Lawrence River with beluga and fin whales. We have navigated international boundaries along the St. Mary's, Pigeon, and Rainy Rivers. In urban places, we are drawn to bridges where we can stand and watch the river flow beneath us, drawing us back through history with images of travelers and traders of long ago.

As canoeists, we love rivers because of where they take us and the freedom they provide. At times we go just to play in the whitewater in much the same way as we delight in a slope of powder snow for telemark skiing. We'll hardly travel any distance but, instead, spend hours and hours catching eddies and surfing waves. That kind of play prepares us for what we love to do best, and that is going on a long journey.

Once you've gained experience and confidence in river travel, you too will feel unlimited by the possibilities presented on the maps. However, as you have discovered, this is not a book about canoe tripping; it is a book of canoe instruction. Before you head out onto the wild blue water, it's important to have a good base of paddling skills. The progression of flatwater skills you've already learned has given you a foundation for paddling on moving water and whitewater. And as you progress, you will discover that your moving water skills will hold you in good stead for lots of rough flatwater conditions.

Moving water and whitewater canoeing demand a combination of river knowledge, technical paddling skill, and experience. On rivers you'll have a chance to use your full repertoire of paddling skills, from paddling to portaging, to lining and tracking the canoe upstream or downstream. Perfect your canoeing skills on flatwater and easy moving water, then choose river runs and rapids to suit your skill level. Then you can be confident that the judgments you make are based on your experience, not someone else's.

River classification is used to give a universal language to describe the difficulties you may face on a river. It is a somewhat subjective guideline, as it is based on judging a river under certain conditions. Flooding, erosion, changing water levels and geological disturbances can completely alter a classificiation. Nothing replaces first-hand experience, even on a familiar river. The classification system is useful in describing a river by rapid or by section but it is rarely used to define the entire river's character. When the water is cold or if the river is remote, a higher rating is given to allow a margin for safety.

International Scale of River Difficulty

Class I, Easy: Easy moving water with riffles or small waves. Any obstructions are obvious and easily avoided. Self-rescue is easy and the risk to swimmers is small.

Class II, Moderate: Wide, clear channels flowing past easily avoided obstructions provide an obvious route for a paddler with some whitewater training. Swimming and self-rescues are straightforward. Experienced paddlers can paddle upstream.

Class III, Difficult: More difficult challenges are presented by the fast current, numerous obstacles and rapids with high, irregular waves that can swamp a canoe. The route is no longer obvious, requiring complex maneuvering down narrow passages. Strainers, holes, big waves, strong eddies and powerful current can all be present, making it necessary for less experienced paddlers to scout from shore and consider portaging.

Class IV, Very Difficult: Precise maneuvering and expert boat control are required to negogiate the turbulent water and to avoid dangerous obstacles. The consequences of mistakes should be considered with a shoreline scout first. The river demands certain moves which, if missed, can result in injurious swims. A foolproof roll and a fast, reliable eddy turn are required as backup for making those "must moves." Considered the limit for open canoes.

Class V, Exceedingly Difficult: These complex, violent and extremely demanding rapids must be scouted from shore. Drops may contain very large, unavoidable waves and holes. Expert rescue skills are required, though rescue itself is very difficult. A foolproof roll is essential, as swimming is highly dangerous.

Class VI, Limit of Navigability: For those who are willing to put life on the edge, as the consequences of mishap can be fatal. The extremely dangerous route is nearing the point of unnavigable and rescues are nearly impossible. This is only for a team of experts who have taken all precautions.

The Magpie flows into the Michipicoten River and on into the northeast corner of Lake Superior.

We urge you to become river watchers. Observe the flow of the water as it moves around river bends, squeezes between rocks, and falls over ledges and boulders. Watch the river in low water and high water as the patterns and formations created around obstacles change. The pattern of currents around obstacles is almost always predictable. Learning to read rivers can be a pastime enjoyed by anyone, paddler or not.

If you have never paddled moving water or whitewater, some of the following maneuvers may look intimidating. Keep in mind that everything shown in the next few chapters is applicable to moving water without any white whatsoever. Flowing water is flowing water, whether fast or slow.

River paddlers have to be adaptable to changing conditions. One day you might be skipping down through a rock garden. Then two days of rain swell the river into a giant lake on the move. Never underestimate the power of moving water. The weight of water is astounding, especially water on the move coming up against a stationary object.

Years ago an upstream capsize against a fallen tree impressed this fact upon me in a truly unforgettable way. I was drifting down the swollen spring waters of the Credit River along with a few paddlers I had recently met. One couple paddled a tandem canoe while the others, including me, paddled whitewater kayaks. At the put-in, I squeezed into my form-fitting, flat-decked little kayak wearing a quarter-inch-thick wetsuit. Because turning around in the kayak felt awkward, I paddled like a horse with blinders on. At one point, I knew I was getting a little ahead of the group, and so looked for a place to wait for them.

But then I made what could have been a fatal decision. I paddled toward a tree overhanging the outside riverbend, where the water flows swiftest. I sensed danger too late and spun away from the main horizontal trunk only to catch my upstream edge. The force of the water flipped and pinned me and my kayak against the log. Suddenly the river carrying me through one of Toronto's wooded valleys was a different creature. Instead of a gentle flow it was an icy torrent. It rushed in on me, tore away my sprayskirt, and flooded the cockpit. A persistent pressure sucked me into the underwater tree limbs where much of the previous year's high-water debris stretched out horizontal like ragged flags in a strong wind.

Fortunately my friends saw the situation and acted quickly. Eddying out behind the tree, they came to my rescue. By this time I could only just get my face above the surface for a breath of air. It took three strong people to pull me away from the river's grasp. My sense of awe and respect for moving water has never diminished from that day.

Whitewater learned solo is enormously fun. Besides that, it helps you become a good tandem canoeing partner.

It is much easier to maneuver a shorter, rockered, whitewater solo canoe than a longer tandem canoe through this rock garden maze on the Pukaskwa River.
Once the decision is made to run such a section of river, river reading on the run becomes an essential skill. Running boulder gardens in a canoe, like running across boulders on your feet, requires you to plan several moves ahead.

14 The River

You can learn a lot about flowing water and its reactions to river obstacles by stepping into a stream less than knee deep. Near shore the water is flowing slower than it is further offshore because the shore provides friction. Even the water near the river bottom flows slower than the water near the surface. Face downstream, with your feet spread a foot apart. Initially the water piles up against your calves, creating pillows of water. Then the current flows to the outside and inside of your legs. Look straight down and you will see the water forms a chute or tongue in the shape of a downstream V. This water speeds up as it passes between your legs, then slows, forming little waves. This is a miniature example of the kind of safe channel that can be run between obstacles in your canoe. The waves are standing waves and the lines that form the V are eddy lines.

The most important aspect of river reading is recognizing eddies. Notice how the water swirls along the eddy lines and then turns upstream to fill in the space in front of your legs. These are eddies. Every river obstruction, be it a rock or a riverbend, has an area of calm water or upstream current behind it.

A paddler reads the river by way of observing the water's reactions to obstacles along its path. You will learn to river read with your eyes as you begin to identify the safe channels, the eddies, the downstream Vs, and the dangers of strainers, hydraulics and undercut rocks. River reading is also learned through experience, by navigating through and playing with these river features. You will even use your ears to help identify potential dangers such as waterfalls. For the full and safe enjoyment of canoeing on moving water, river reading is an essential skill worth mastering.

A skillful canoeist can save time and effort by scouting the route from the canoe. However, there are situations where scouting from shore is the safest idea. Scout as close to the rapids as possible, not on a cliff overlooking the river. Plan your route through the rapid by looking back upstream. Look downstream and note key markers on shore and in the river that will enable you to find your bearings once you are back in the canoe galloping through the whitewater.

River Left and River Right

"Left" and "right" can be confusing terms, and that is why we have consistently used onside and offside to describe a paddler's body in relation to the paddle, and to describe strokes and maneuvers in relation to the side a paddler is paddling on. Now that we are on the river, we find more possibilities for confusion with the river banks. To simplify the matter, the two sides of the river will always be defined as *river left* and *river right* as you look downstream. No matter how you are viewing the river — upstream, downstream, or standing on your head — river left and river right are fixed by this downstream perspective.

Scout the River

- If you are a novice and want to plan your route more carefully.
- If the water level has risen overnight, changing the conditions.
- If it is spring or there are flood-level conditions where strainers are a danger.
- If you hear a lot of water noise ahead and you can see the river drops out of sight over a ledge.

River Features

Channel: *Often the deepest and fastest current, where a significant volume of the river water flows.*

Eddies: *Eddies are found along the shore and in mid-river behind everything from riverbends to rocks. An obstacle, be it at the surface or underwater, diverts the water past it. The void created downstream of the obstacle is filled by an upstream current. Wherever the water flows upstream relative to the main current, an eddy has been created. There are different kinds of eddies.*

Downstream V: *When the river flows through two surface features, the water is deflected off them, forming eddy lines in the shape of a V with the apex facing downstream. The chute, or tongue, of faster water lying between the V is very often the safe channel to run.*

Cross Section of a Straight River with Typical Current Speeds

slowest   fastest current   slowest

slower

river left

river flow

downstream V

shoreline eddy

river right

channel

drop

hydraulic

Low Head Dam or Manmade Weir

Falls: *A steep drop in which water falls freely part of the way down. For a paddler, the warning signs can be the roar of water, the sight of mist, and the apparent straight horizon line between the river and the sky or downstream scenery. Scout from shore!*

Low head dam or manmade weir: *These unassuming manmade drops are extremely dangerous, and life-threatening should you get caught in one. If the dam extends from shore to shore, then the resultant hydraulic found below the dam is the ultimate keeper. There is no break in the deep reversal for a recirculating swimmer to swim free.*

120

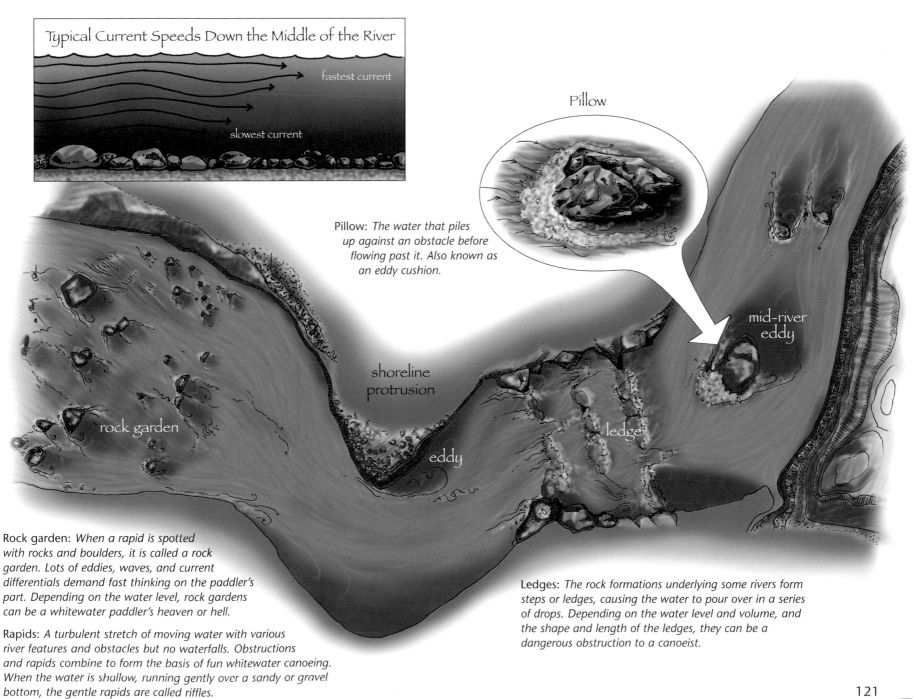

Typical Current Speeds Down the Middle of the River

fastest current

slowest current

Pillow

Pillow: *The water that piles up against an obstacle before flowing past it. Also known as an eddy cushion.*

mid-river eddy

shoreline protrusion

rock garden

eddy

ledge

Rock garden: *When a rapid is spotted with rocks and boulders, it is called a rock garden. Lots of eddies, waves, and current differentials demand fast thinking on the paddler's part. Depending on the water level, rock gardens can be a whitewater paddler's heaven or hell.*

Rapids: *A turbulent stretch of moving water with various river features and obstacles but no waterfalls. Obstructions and rapids combine to form the basis of fun whitewater canoeing. When the water is shallow, running gently over a sandy or gravel bottom, the gentle rapids are called riffles.*

Ledges: *The rock formations underlying some rivers form steps or ledges, causing the water to pour over in a series of drops. Depending on the water level and volume, and the shape and length of the ledges, they can be a dangerous obstruction to a canoeist.*

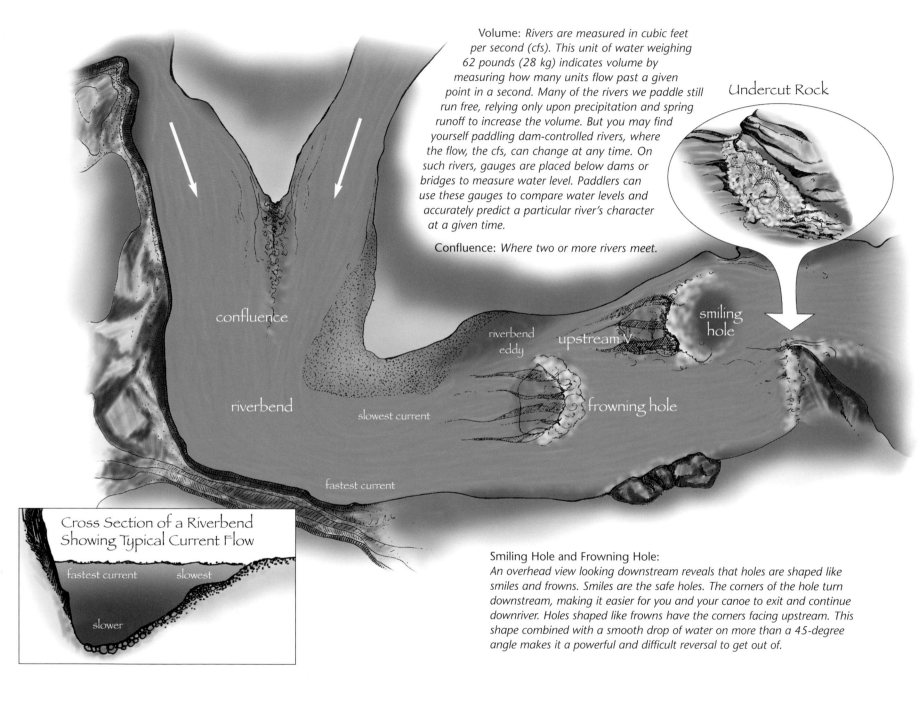

Volume: *Rivers are measured in cubic feet per second (cfs). This unit of water weighing 62 pounds (28 kg) indicates volume by measuring how many units flow past a given point in a second. Many of the rivers we paddle still run free, relying only upon precipitation and spring runoff to increase the volume. But you may find yourself paddling dam-controlled rivers, where the flow, the cfs, can change at any time. On such rivers, gauges are placed below dams or bridges to measure water level. Paddlers can use these gauges to compare water levels and accurately predict a particular river's character at a given time.*

Confluence: *Where two or more rivers meet.*

Undercut Rock

confluence

riverbend

slowest current

fastest current

riverbend eddy

upstream V

smiling hole

frowning hole

Cross Section of a Riverbend
Showing Typical Current Flow

fastest current   slowest

slower

Smiling Hole and Frowning Hole:
An overhead view looking downstream reveals that holes are shaped like smiles and frowns. Smiles are the safe holes. The corners of the hole turn downstream, making it easier for you and your canoe to exit and continue downriver. Holes shaped like frowns have the corners facing upstream. This shape combined with a smooth drop of water on more than a 45-degree angle makes it a powerful and difficult reversal to get out of.

Chute: *When the river is compressed between two or more obstacles, it speeds up. (See Downstream V). This smooth, dark chute, also referred to as a tongue, often indicates the safe channel for a paddler to follow.*

Stoppers: *These are small holes that can halt your canoe briefly but they won't hold it because too much water is flowing downstream through the reversal.*

Strainers and Sweepers: *Water flowing through the branches of a fallen tree represents one of the most serious hazards for a canoeist. These giant strainers act like the kitchen sieve, allowing water through but capturing canoes, paddles, and paddlers — which can be fatal. Give strainers a wide berth!*

stopper

strainer/ sweeper

Standing Waves

eddy

trough crest

chute

standing waves

eddy

Trough: *The hollow between the crests of two waves.*

Eddy wall: *When the current differentials are extreme, a wall of water forms between the eddy and the main current near the obstacle that is creating the eddy.*

Boil: *This feature literally looks like a bubble in thick boiling liquid. Boils rise in places where there are underwater obstructions or the current slows down. They are found downstream of undercut rocks, which can be a hidden danger to unsuspecting canoeists.*

Upstream V: *When the river hits an obstacle, it diverges from this point, creating an upstream V with the object being at the apex of the V. You want to avoid upstream Vs.*

Eddy Wall

Standing waves: *These waves occur when the faster moving water hits slower moving water. Standing waves, otherwise known as haystacks, remain stationary while the water flows through them. The height of these waves is measured from crest to trough.*

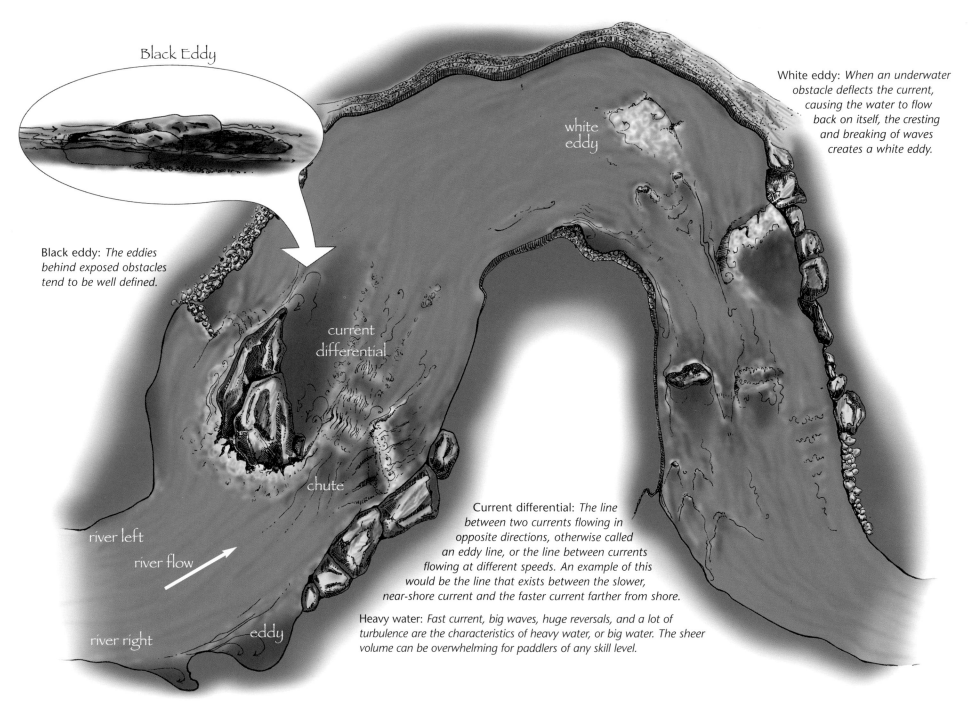

Black Eddy

White eddy: *When an underwater obstacle deflects the current, causing the water to flow back on itself, the cresting and breaking of waves creates a white eddy.*

white eddy

Black eddy: *The eddies behind exposed obstacles tend to be well defined.*

current differential

chute

river left

river flow

river right

eddy

Current differential: *The line between two currents flowing in opposite directions, otherwise called an eddy line, or the line between currents flowing at different speeds. An example of this would be the line that exists between the slower, near-shore current and the faster current farther from shore.*

Heavy water: *Fast current, big waves, huge reversals, and a lot of turbulence are the characteristics of heavy water, or big water. The sheer volume can be overwhelming for paddlers of any skill level.*

Reversals: *When the water falls over a drop or obstruction, it loses speed and falls back on itself to fill the trough. Reversals can be fun and they can be dangerous, depending on their size, shape, and holding power. From a paddler's point of view, stoppers are fun but hydraulics and keepers are to be avoided.*

Hydraulics: *These are powerful recirculating currents created below ledges, rocks, or manmade weirs. The eddy behind a hydraulic is obvious. If the water is being drawn into a hole from more than 4 feet (100 cm) away, stay away; otherwise you may get pulled in and find it difficult to escape. These very large holes are called keepers.*

Surfing wave: *Canoeists can ride the upstream face of a standing wave. While gravity pulls the canoe into the trough, the current tries to force it up and over the crest. The resulting dynamic equilibrium creates an amazing whitewater playboating river feature.*

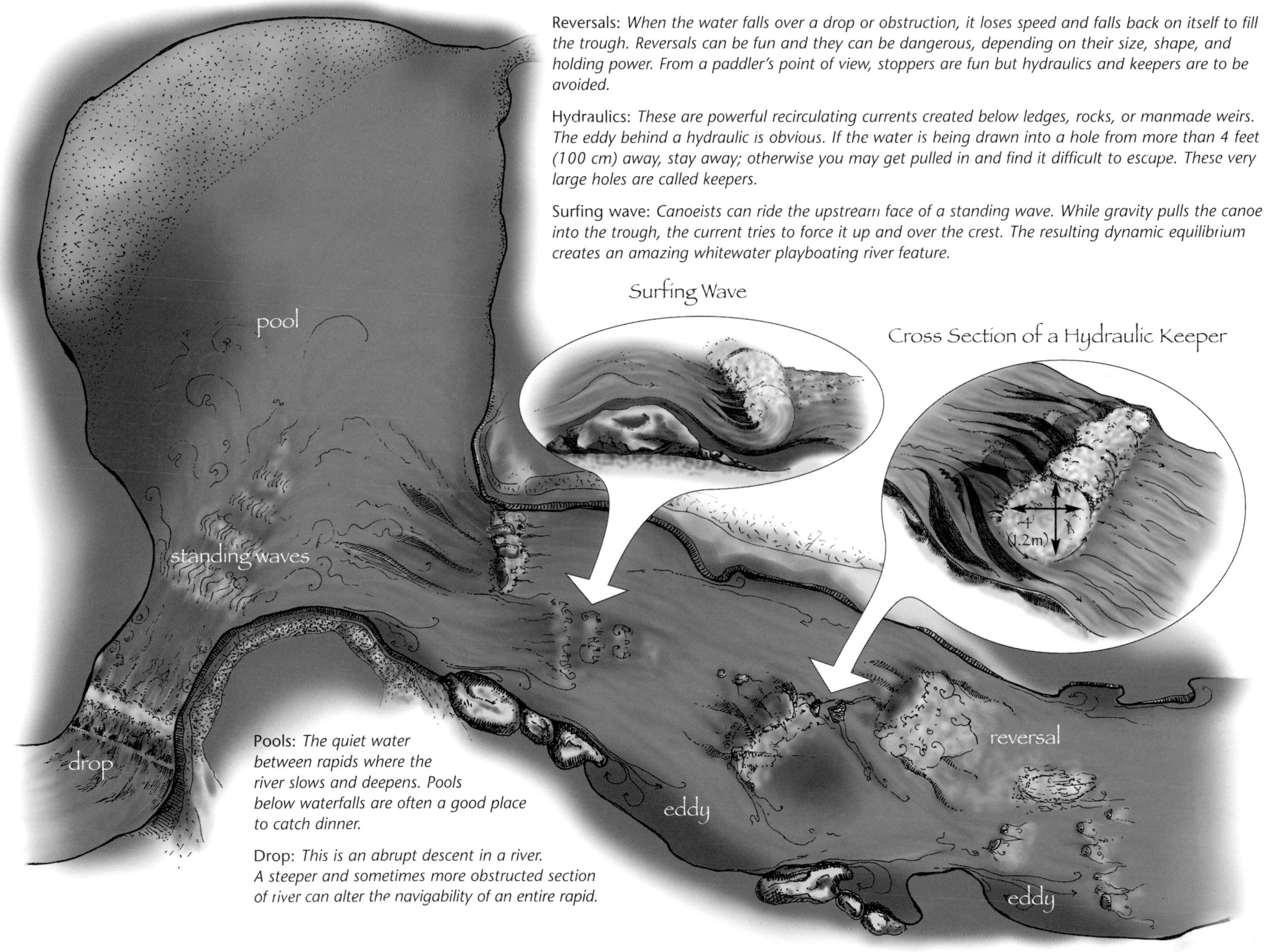

Surfing Wave

Cross Section of a Hydraulic Keeper

4' (1.2m)

pool

standing waves

drop

Pools: *The quiet water between rapids where the river slows and deepens. Pools below waterfalls are often a good place to catch dinner.*

Drop: *This is an abrupt descent in a river. A steeper and sometimes more obstructed section of river can alter the navigability of an entire rapid.*

eddy

reversal

eddy

15 Preparing for the River

In learning the art of whitewater paddling, your efforts will be greatly enhanced in a fully outfitted whitewater canoe. Just as a snug-fitting ski boot allows a skier to have excellent edge control on the slopes, a properly fitted canoe allows a paddler excellent control in whitewater. Turning, bracing, edging, and righting the canoe can be performed with the most efficiency when the paddler's knees are held securely on the bottom of the canoe. A well-outfitted canoe also makes the 360-degree roll possible. In whitewater, critical timing and precise control are necessary when you sideslip within a hair's breadth of a rock or carve that turn into a must-catch eddy. Flotation displaces a very heavy load of water, making the canoe lighter and more responsive in the event of a capsize. The canoe is less dangerous and easier to rescue, and impacts with obstacles are not as severe.

Outfitting Your Whitewater Canoe

1 *A whitewater canoe outfitted with a pedestal seat, thigh straps, knee cups, and toe blocks allows a paddler to be well connected to the canoe. Thigh straps secure a paddler's knees to the canoe for good boat control. The exact placement of the straps is important. They should apply pressure on the thighs without slipping off, but at the same time allow an easy wet exit. Knee cups stabilize your knees by preventing them from slipping sideways. To keep your thighs under the straps, place the balls of your feet on the foot braces. These can be either fixed or adjustable, and they are important for holding your thighs under the straps, especially when rolling.*

2 *We outfit all of our canoes with a grab loop–painter system. The painters can be easily unfurled for lining, tracking, tethering, and rescue work. When not in use, they are safely stowed so as not to cause entanglement. Grab loops attached to the bow and stern are made by threading a rope through the hull and tying it with a fisherman's knot (see Chapter 22). Painters (ropes) approximately 10 feet (3 m) long are attached with a bowline or figure-eight knot to the bow and stern grab loops. These ropes should be highly visible, flotable, and neatly tucked under a bungee cord on each deck plate.*

4   A serrated, stainless-steel knife is safely stored but easily deployed from the harness sheath. You might need it to rescue yourself or another paddler from rope entanglement. Attach a loud whistle to your zipper slider. (Make sure it works in cold, wet conditions.)

5   A harness is incorporated into the design of this whitewater PFD, adding to its versatility in rescue situations. The closed-cell foam panels provide greater flotation and warmth, and they protect your body from impact with rocks. It is a good idea to have a throwbag with you at all times while river paddling. This jacket incorporates a back pouch for carrying the rope, thus freeing up your hands. A strap allows one-handed access.

6   Knowing how and where to use a rescue rope is just as important as carrying one. On dry land, practice accuracy by throwing it at a moving target — like a running friend. On the water, forewarn a swimmer that you are about to throw a rope by blowing your whistle or yelling "Rope!"

7   All whitewater paddlers should wear a comfortable Coast Guard-approved, Type III personal flotation device (PFD). Adjustable side straps ensure a snug fit over a T-shirt or a cold-weather layering system.

River Signals

The river can be a noisy place. Body language and the use of a very loud whistle are the best ways to attract the attention of other paddlers. Before heading down any river, it is wise to make sure every member of the group knows these universally accepted signals. When you receive a signal, you should repeat it back to the sender to let him know that you have understood correctly. Good communication can prevent accidents, and it can speed up emergency response. Messages can be passed back up the river to other paddlers in the group by repeating the signals. When passing a signal on to another paddler, be sure to do it where it has meaning for the receiver.

When using a signal to indicate the routes to be followed, *always point toward the course that should be taken by the paddlers you are assisting, never at the obstacle*. It is always wise with a group to establish a river running plan. A lead canoe containing an experienced paddler sets the pace and the general course, communicates the plan, and scouts if necessary. The group is followed by a designated sweep boat, which carries first-aid and repair supplies, and also holds the responsibility of keeping the group intact.

1 *All clear: If one of these signals is given, it indicates all clear to proceed and indicates a preferred route. From left to right, these signals read "run river left," "run center," and "run river right." Turn the paddle blade flat so it can be seen easily from a distance. Always point toward the safe route, never toward the hazard.*

2   *Help/Emergency: Three long blasts on a loud whistle while waving a paddle, helmet, lifejacket, or brightly colored throwbag over your head indicates that you need help as quickly as possible. A whistle can be heard over the river's roar, but if you don't have one, use the visual signal alone. Attach the whistle on the zipper slider of your lifejacket for quick use.*

3   *Stop: Wave your horizontally outstretched arms up and down to warn other paddlers that there is a potential hazard ahead. The signal can be repeated and passed along. Wait for the all-clear signal to proceed.*

4   *Stop: Another way to warn others of potential hazards ahead is to hold the paddle horizontally and pump it up and down. The signal should be repeated and passed along to other paddlers. Scout the route or wait for the all-clear signal before proceeding.*

16 Balancing for the River

Once you have learned how to "wear" the canoe, you have a lot more control when it comes to edging, balance, and recovery. You can also take full advantage of the canoe's inherent turning capability. Here are a few exercises you can practice to get better acquainted with the feel of an outfitted canoe: gunwale bobbing for balance, righting exercises for confidence, and spins for maneuverability and edge control.

Gunwale Bobbing

Gunwale bobbing is a canoe game we played as children — and one we still play. The idea is for two paddlers to stand, balanced on the gunwales, one at the bow, the other at the stern, at about where the seats are located. Bend and straighten your knees to set the canoe bobbing. The idea is to unbalance your opponent, sending him in for a swim. Rubber-soled booties are ideal for preventing your feet from slipping on the gunwales, but generations of paddlers have played this game in bare feet.

Practice Righting Strokes

1 *Here's one way to work with your paddling partner to develop good reflexes for your righting strokes. One person stands in the water at the stern of the canoe while the other sits in the canoe, paddle in the ready position.*

2 *The person in the water gives the canoe a sudden hearty twist to one side or the other, bringing the gunwale to the water.*

3 *The canoeist cannot see when or which way this is going to happen, so he develops an automatic and effective reflex to avoid a capsize. This exercise also encourages a "don't ever give up" attitude.*

1 *One good exercise for learning the extremes of your properly outfitted whitewater canoe is to repeatedly edge the canoe past the point of capsize and then right it again using righting strokes: the low brace (shown here) or the righting pry.*

2 *To review the righting strokes, see pages 40–41 in Chapter 7, Getting Centered. When you are held in the canoe with thigh straps and foot braces, you have greater control. For instance, you are now able to forcefully lift your onside knee to assist the righting action.*

3 *When you perform the low brace, remember to get both hands wet and hit the water with the entire backface of the blade. Throw your head down; this will cause you to lift up with your onside knee and push down with your offside knee. Sit up only when your head and upper body have swung past the centerline.*

1 *Rotate your onside shoulder back and lean back slightly. Your hands are over the water. Maintain a low shaft-angle. Plant the blade near the stern, holding it on a climbing angle.*

2 *Keep the blade on this climbing angle as you apply pressure. Your thigh straps will greatly assist in raising the canoe's side of opposition. Weight the onside knee as before and lift with the offside knee.*

3 *By the time the paddle shaft is at right angles to the centerline, you will be sitting up straight. Continue rotating your onside shoulder forward as you apply pressure to the blade. Weight your offside knee.*

4 *By the time the bow comes to the blade, you should be leaning forward slightly, with the onside slightly raised. Exit the blade smoothly by turning your control thumb back to prepare for the recovery.*

5 *To recover, rotate your onside shoulder back again, feathering the blade on a climbing angle. Lean back slightly at the catch. Spin again and again.*

Spins in a Solo Whitewater Canoe

Back on pages 44–47, we demonstrated how sweeps are used to spin a solo canoe. If you compare those images with these shown here, you can see how the ease of spinning changes with different hull shapes. The straighter keel line of a flatwater canoe has to be edged a fair bit to achieve more rocker, but even then the straight stems keep you from achieving a smooth spin. A rockered whitewater canoe spins on a dime. One sweep turns you 180 degrees. This is to the whitewater canoeist's advantage, since you are always turning on the river.

Edge the canoe toward the blade at the beginning of the stroke and away from it at the end of the stroke. Follow the movement with your body by leaning forward at the hips then leaning back at the end of the stroke. Once you are in a fully outfitted canoe with thigh straps, toe blocks, and saddles, you are wearing the boat. By wearing it, you can lift the side of opposition, that is, the side moving against the water, rather than just weighting and unweighting your knees as you did on flatwater. The idea is to make repeated reverse sweeps for onside spins and repeated forward sweeps for offside spins, concentrating on good torso rotation, edge control, and watching the force of water on the paddle blade.

In the rush and tumble of whitewater, the river's voice dominates, so paddlers use a system of river signals to speak to one another. Below the drop, a raised paddle held straight up indicates to the canoeist above that the way is all clear and to make the run down the center of the river.

The Solo Start-up

The ability to go from a dead stop to an immediate fast forward in a straight line is an important skill for a whitewater paddler to develop. When you cross eddy lines, it is momentum that helps you control the angle of your canoe. Controlling your angle is particularly important for ferrying, surfing, and upstream paddling.

Practice your *solo start-up* on flatwater. Select a target and turn the bow 45 degrees toward your onside, away from this target. (Keep in mind that 45 degrees is an approximate angle. It will vary depending on the strength of your forward stroke and the shape of your canoe's hull.) Take one well-executed forward stroke then immediately follow it with two cross forward strokes. The canoe will be turning slightly toward your onside. This sets up your inside circle, something you will learn about in the next chapter. The important thing is that you are headed on a relatively straight trajectory toward the target as you follow up on the two cross forwards with a forward stroke. You have now effectively attained a straight-line paddling maximum speed, all within a very short distance, without using any corrective strokes.

1 *Aim the bow of the canoe 45 degrees away from your target, toward your onside. Take a forward stroke.*

2 *The forward stroke swings the bow to the offside, toward your target. Take your first of two cross forward strokes.*

3 *Take the second cross forward stroke. This sets up the natural path of the canoe's inside circle. (See Chapter 17, Paddling in Circles and Arcs.)*

4 The canoe is now traveling on the arc of the inside circle. Edge the canoe toward your onside, which means you are edging toward the inside of the circle.

5 You have brought the canoe to full speed without using any corrective strokes, using only power strokes to reach your target.

Gateway to the North

The idea of paddling a river efficiently can be a metaphor for many things, but let's compare it for the moment to reading a Robert Service poem aloud. The rhyming words roll off the tongue without any effort at all. The words have a rhythm that is, to me, comparable to your paddle strokes. The "poem" of the river run is punctuated by eddy turns and peel-outs. We think of running a complex rapid fluidly as "poetry in motion."

This exercise, which uses two marker buoys, is a way of increasing your speed and efficiency while fine tuning and minimizing your strokes. Our British paddling friends call it the wiggle test. With some adaptations for open canoeing, we call it the Gateway to the North.

Make Your Own Gateway to the North

Take two 5-foot (1.5 m) pieces of 3/4-inch (2 cm) galvanized iron water-pipe. One pipe anchors your buoys to the lake or pond bottom while the other pipe, also horizontal, suspended 3 feet (90 cm) below the surface, acts as a spacer bar maintaining the distance between the buoys (and preventing the buoys from drifting together or apart).

Drill four holes, one hole close to the ends of each bar. Lay the two pipes on the ground horizontal to one another. Pretend the first bar is lying on the lake bottom. Now consider your depth and place the spacer bar parallel to the lake-bottom bar so it is approximately 3 feet (90 cm) from the surface.

Take two pieces of nylon cord longer than the depth of the water. Put a knot in the end of each one. Thread one cord through the hole in the right-hand end of the lake-bottom bar and the second cord through the hole in the left-hand end of that bar. Tie a knot in each cord at the point where it would be 3 feet (90 cm) from the surface. These knots prevent the spacer bar from sliding down the cords to the lake bottom. Thread each of the two cords through the holes in the ends of the spacer bar. Tie the loose ends to your buoys.

Practicing with the Gateway to the North

For this diagram, the buoys have been made larger and placed
further apart than they actually are (see facing page).

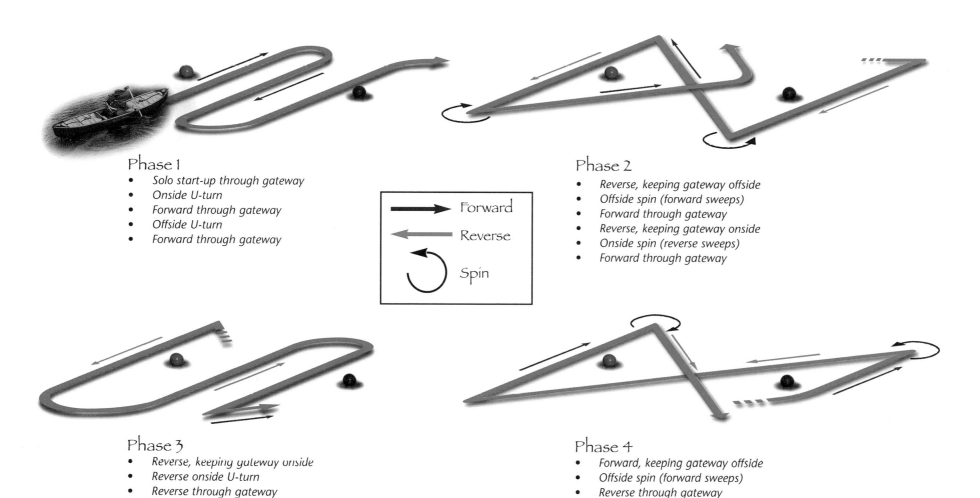

Phase 1
- *Solo start-up through gateway*
- *Onside U-turn*
- *Forward through gateway*
- *Offside U-turn*
- *Forward through gateway*

→ Forward

← Reverse

↻ Spin

Phase 2
- *Reverse, keeping gateway offside*
- *Offside spin (forward sweeps)*
- *Forward through gateway*
- *Reverse, keeping gateway onside*
- *Onside spin (reverse sweeps)*
- *Forward through gateway*

Phase 3
- *Reverse, keeping gateway onside*
- *Reverse onside U-turn*
- *Reverse through gateway*
- *Reverse offside U-turn*
- *Reverse through gateway*

Phase 4
- *Forward, keeping gateway offside*
- *Offside spin (forward sweeps)*
- *Reverse through gateway*
- *Forward, keeping gateway onside*
- *Onside spin*
- *Reverse through gateway*

17 Paddling in Circles and Arcs

Every canoe has a natural tendency to turn when a forward stroke is taken simply because the forward stroke is made on one side of the canoe or the other and not down the centerline. Paddling on the circumference of a circle in an arc rather than in a straight line provides a canoeist in a rockered whitewater canoe with a more efficient way of getting from one place to another. Understanding this approach to paddling whitewater is fundamental to every eddy turn, peel-out, C-turn, ferry, and S-turn demonstrated in Chapter 18.

Once some forward momentum has been achieved in a flatwater canoe, the straight stem continues to slice a path while the straight keel line follows in this path. If your paddling technique is efficient, you will need minimal corrective strokes to keep the flatwater canoe on

course. Straight-ahead movement is also helped by the even water pressure on both sides of the frontal-resistance (leading) end of the canoe. In whitewater paddling, the ability to change direction outweighs the need to track a straight line, and so the canoe's tracking characteristics are sacrificed for more maneuverability.

The hull of a modern whitewater canoe is highly rockered. For a beginner, the inherent tendency of this hull design to turn can make paddling one a real challenge. The continuous use of corrective strokes takes time and slows the canoe down. Learning to paddle the *inside circle,* which is actually paddling on the inside of the circle carved by the canoe, transforms this tendency to turn into forward propulsion. This power greatly enhances your ability to control your canoe.

The technique of paddling the inside circle involves using the forward and cross forward strokes in the leading (frontal-resistance) end of the canoe. It also involves modifying your forward stroke by placing the blade further from the hull to decrease the canoe's tendency to turn in a tight circle. This stroke is called the *forward control*

stroke. A canoe carves two inside circles: one on your onside, when you are using forward strokes, and one on your offside, when using cross forward strokes. You have to get up some momentum, edge the canoe toward the turn, and paddle on the inside of the circle. To initiate the inside circle if you are beginning from a dead stop, use the solo start-up, as shown on page 136.

Keep paddling forward and the canoe will stay on the arc of the circle. Once you are "on the circle," you can vary the size of the circle by increasing or decreasing edging, and forward stroking closer to or further from the centerline. To make the circle larger, place your blade further from the hull as you take forward or cross forward strokes (these are forward control strokes) and edge the canoe less. This large circle effectively creates a straight-line path for river paddling. To make the circle smaller, edge the canoe more and place the blade closer to the centerline as you take your forward or cross forward strokes.

The following six photos demonstrate paddling an inside circle on the paddler's onside. So we say he is paddling an *onside circle.*

The Onside Circle

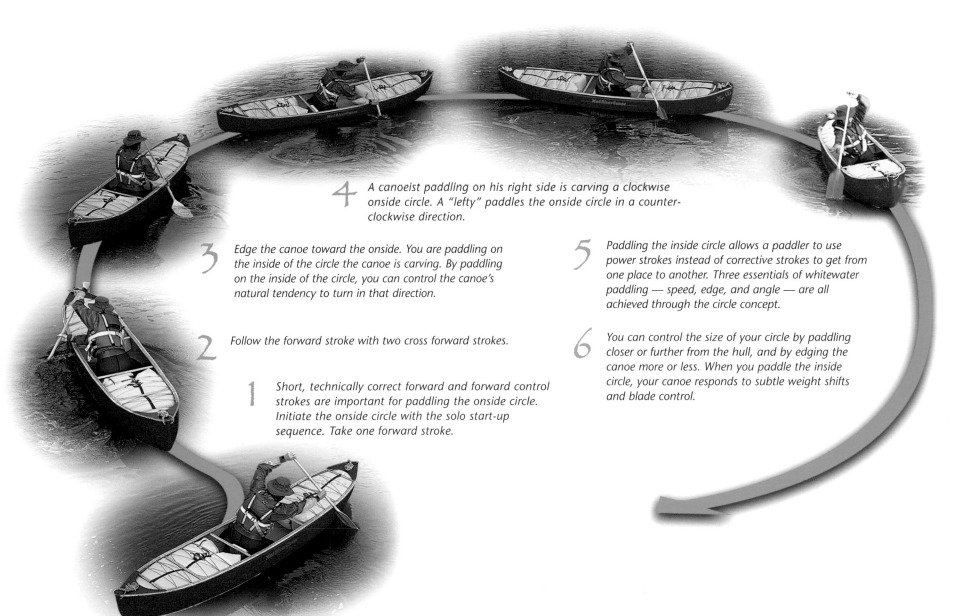

4 A canoeist paddling on his right side is carving a clockwise onside circle. A "lefty" paddles the onside circle in a counter-clockwise direction.

3 Edge the canoe toward the onside. You are paddling on the inside of the circle the canoe is carving. By paddling on the inside of the circle, you can control the canoe's natural tendency to turn in that direction.

2 Follow the forward stroke with two cross forward strokes.

1 Short, technically correct forward and forward control strokes are important for paddling the onside circle. Initiate the onside circle with the solo start-up sequence. Take one forward stroke.

5 Paddling the inside circle allows a paddler to use power strokes instead of corrective strokes to get from one place to another. Three essentials of whitewater paddling — speed, edge, and angle — are all achieved through the circle concept.

6 You can control the size of your circle by paddling closer or further from the hull, and by edging the canoe more or less. When you paddle the inside circle, your canoe responds to subtle weight shifts and blade control.

The Offside Circle

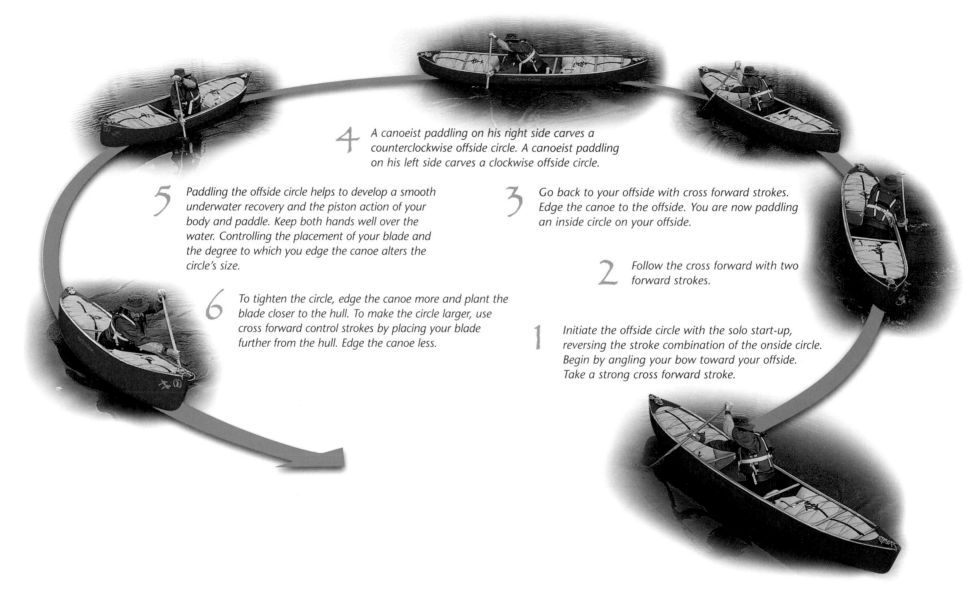

4 A canoeist paddling on his right side carves a counterclockwise offside circle. A canoeist paddling on his left side carves a clockwise offside circle.

5 Paddling the offside circle helps to develop a smooth underwater recovery and the piston action of your body and paddle. Keep both hands well over the water. Controlling the placement of your blade and the degree to which you edge the canoe alters the circle's size.

3 Go back to your offside with cross forward strokes. Edge the canoe to the offside. You are now paddling an inside circle on your offside.

2 Follow the cross forward with two forward strokes.

6 To tighten the circle, edge the canoe more and plant the blade closer to the hull. To make the circle larger, use cross forward control strokes by placing your blade further from the hull. Edge the canoe less.

1 Initiate the offside circle with the solo start-up, reversing the stroke combination of the onside circle. Begin by angling your bow toward your offside. Take a strong cross forward stroke.

The Cross Forward Sweep

This stroke enables you to make a quick and smooth transition from an offside to an onside circle. On your offside, place your blade as close to the bow as possible. Choke up with your shaft hand and maintain a low shaft-angle. Lean forward and turn the canoe away from the blade, bringing your torso to an upright position as you do so. At the end of the stroke, turn your control thumb forward and feather the blade all the way across to your onside, going right into forward strokes. In other words, one *cross forward sweep* should be all that is necessary to set you up for your onside circle.

Paddling the Inside Circle on the River

Paddling in all those circles may have made you dizzy but, like Dorothy in *The Wizard of Oz,* you have been transformed. Never again will you see your river paths as point-to-point arrow-straight freeways. Instead you will paddle in a series of graceful curves emulating the natural flow of the river itself.

The next step is to progress from paddling circles on flatwater to paddling circles on moving water without obstacles. Begin by paddling your inside circle, being aware of the fact that the forces acting upon the canoe will change depending on whether you face upstream or downstream. Paddling the inside circle is not the same as pirouetting on the river with spins. You now have forward momentum, so when you are facing downstream, your circle will open up because there is less pressure on the leading end of the canoe (the bow). You will have to edge the canoe more to carve the circle. But when you are facing upstream, the water pressure against the leading end (the bow) will force a tight circle that you will have to resist by executing forward control strokes further out from the hull to open up the circle.

Challenge yourself to think about what is happening between the canoe and the current. In any sport, it is both fun and instructive to develop a sensitivity for why things happen. Only then are you consistently able to repeat the maneuver.

Figure Eight Exercise

Once you have practiced paddling the inside circle on your onside and offside, separately increasing and decreasing the size of the circles, it's time to stitch them together in a figure eight. Efficient river running and playboating demands that you be constantly moving from one circle to the other, one arc to another. There are various ways of making a smooth transition from your onside circle to your offside circle and back again. Here's what we do.

To change from your onside to your offside circle, weight your offside knee to level the canoe. At the same time, take a couple of forward control strokes, with the blade held away from the hull. You can use a forward sweep to get the canoe moving toward the offside.

If you are paddling on your offside circle and you wish to move to your onside circle, level the canoe by weighting your onside knee and take cross forward control strokes (further from the hull) or one cross forward sweep.

Late-summer surfing on the Magnetawan River. This waterway is a longtime friend that we return to visit as often as we can.

Rivers are stories flowing through the land; when we join them we are bound for a great and mysterious adventure.
Be bold but respectful, for the flow of water is one of the most powerful forces on Earth.

18 Whitewater Maneuvers

ddy turns, peel-outs, and ferries are the three basic maneuvers you perform on moving water to dance down the river. The *eddy turn* is a U-turn on moving water, a maneuver that allows you to catch or enter an eddy. A *peel-out* is the U-turn maneuver you use to exit an eddy and enter the main downstream current. *Ferrying* is a maneuver that enables you to travel laterally across the current. The three work together in a variety of combinations creating C-turns and S-turns.

Once again, think for a moment of the canoe in terms of its leading (frontal-resistance) end and its following (eddy-resistance) end rather than the bow and stern. All three of these moves can be performed facing upstream or downstream, backward or forward. All that really matters are three factors: speed, edge, and angle. Remember the SEA!

Speed is the necessary velocity of the canoe to cross the eddy line. *Edge* causes the canoe to carve in the direction of the turn. *Angle* refers to the orientation of the canoe in relationship to the entering or leaving current.

Entering current and *leaving current* are universal terms defining where the canoe is in relation to the *eddy line* that divides the opposing currents. When the canoe is about to cross this eddy line, or current differential, we say it is in the leaving current and heading for the entering current.

SEA

Speed, Edge, Angle. We find the acronym SEA (think of *Paddle-to-the-Sea*) is an easy way to remember the key ingredients to leaving and entering eddies. In order to be in control you need to be traveling faster than the leaving current, you need to be edging in the direction you are turning, and you must be angled correctly to the current.

Tandem Onside Eddy Turn Using a Duffek

1   Prepare for the eddy turn well in advance of reaching the eddy. Begin carving the inside circle toward the top of the eddy, setting both edge and angle. By paddling the inside circle, both paddlers can contribute to forward momentum, especially while crossing the eddy line. The challenge to catching eddies is in aiming at a stationary object while you move. Hit the eddy too high and you hit the rock that created it. Hit the eddy too low and you risk missing the eddy altogether.

2   *The canoe crosses the eddy line on an angle of 45 degrees or greater. The differential between the main current and the eddy is what spins the canoe. The greater the difference, the quicker you will turn. If, for instance, the main downstream current is 7 mph (12 kph) and the upstream current in the eddy is 2 mph (3 kph), the total torque on the leading end of the canoe when it crosses the line is 9 mph (14 kph). This is why it is imperative for the canoe to already be edging and angling in the direction of the turn before the bow paddler plants the stroke around which the canoe turns. It doesn't matter what kind of stroke the bow paddler places in the eddy; if the canoe is edged and angled inappropriately (angled downstream or edged to the wrong side), a human holding a paddle is no match for the tremendous force of the water acting on the surface of the canoe.*

3   *The bow paddler places a Duffek in the entering current, that is, the eddy, and draws the bow to the planted paddle. The stern paddler assists with stern sweeps. Two things happen when the bow hits the eddy line. First, the upstream current in the eddy grabs the bow, spinning the canoe around to face upstream. Second, the upstream current in the eddy tugs at the bottom of the canoe. If you don't compensate with proper edging, the canoe can be swiftly slipped out from beneath you.*

4   *Once in the eddy, it is important to continue edging in the direction of the turn. Wait for the bow to meet the planted Duffek. Once in the eddy you can either stop, rest, and scout, or continue paddling up the eddy and back out into the current. If the eddy is small and you are in a tandem canoe, hold the bow at the top of the eddy so you don't accidentally find yourself drifting out of the bottom of it.*

To review this maneuver on flatwater, see the Tandem Onside U-Turn Using a Duffek, on pages 86–87.

Tandem Onside Eddy Turn Using a Compound Reverse Sweep

1. You need speed to catch eddies so, while in the main current, paddle hard. Plan well in advance for the next eddy, aiming for the top of it, where the eddy line is most defined. Before crossing the eddy line, consider your speed, edge, and angle.

2. Hitting the top of the eddy on a 45-degree angle or greater takes practice. The acute angle is important because the water along the top of the eddy line flows faster than the main current as it passes the obstacle. This rejector line will deflect your canoe back into the main current if you don't have enough angle and speed.

3. The bow paddler places a compound reverse sweep as the anchor. When the first part of this stroke is placed in the entering current (the eddy), the canoe makes a crisp turn because the compound reverse sweep actually puts the brakes on. This is very useful if you enter the eddy too quickly and are going to hit shore, or if the eddy is shallow and you can't plant a Duffek, or if you have so much momentum entering a small mid-river eddy that you might shoot right through it and out the other side.

4. Both paddlers hold the edge into the turn as the bow swings upstream toward the bow paddler's anchored paddle. The stern paddler assists by providing more turning momentum with stern sweeps. Capsizes in eddies usually happen because the canoe is leveled out before the stern has finished skidding laterally into the eddy. The stern is in a sort of crack-the-whip situation, with the bow hanging on to that anchor point. The bow paddler transforms his compound reverse sweep into a forward stroke. The stern paddler follows through with forward strokes.

To review this maneuver on flatwater, see the Tandem Onside U-Turn Using a Compound Reverse Sweep, on pages 88–89.

Advanced Tandem Offside Eddy Turn

An advanced eddy turn (not shown) can be made using the sliding pry and slice as shown on pages 84–85 in Chapter 10. If you are going to try this, be aware that you need a *deep water eddy* and nerves of steel.

The stern paddler must be ready when the bow paddler places the sliding pry. You will know if you are J-leaning properly. If your center of balance is not over the canoe's centerline when the canoe is edged to the outside of the turn, the bow paddler will go flying out of the canoe. This turn breaks the cardinal rule of always edging in the direction of your turn.

This turn is extremely fast and exciting because the bow's turning momentum is enhanced by the force of the water against the backface of the blade. The stern paddler does a reverse sweeping low brace, which also helps bring the canoe around with speed. The bow paddler slides the pry up to the bow and immediately draws back with a forward slice, while the stern paddler turns his reverse sweeping low brace into a forward stroke.

This maneuver can also be used as an advanced tandem offside peel-out with one main exception. Follow the cardinal rule and edge the canoe in the direction of the turn.

One important paddling skill not always so easily learned is judgment. What are you capable of running? When do you decide to portage instead? Today's superb whitewater outfitting can improve your skills and certainly increases safety, but remember, your body is not as tough as Royalex. Consider your well being and that of your fellow paddlers first.

Originating in the Algonquin Highlands in Ontario's oldest provincial park, the Magnetawan River flows west to Georgian Bay. En route, the river presents a steady progression of new challenges, making it ideal for paddlers with some whitewater experience.

Solo Onside Peel-out

1 Use the solo start-up to get going. It should take no more than three strokes to establish the necessary speed for crossing the eddy line.

2 The peel-out, like the eddy turn, requires speed, edge, and angle (SEA). Once you have forward momentum, edge the canoe into the turn (remember your J-lean) and set the angle before crossing the eddy line into the main downstream current (the entering current).

3 Place the Duffek in the entering current. Your onside knee is weighted and your body should be in the J-lean position. This means you have an upright upper body and you are not leaning on your paddle.

4 The Duffek is the anchor around which the canoe turns. Bring the bow to the paddle blade and then follow through with a forward stroke.

5 Maintain forward momentum to keep you moving into your next maneuver.

To review this maneuver on flatwater, see the Solo Onside U-Turn Using a Duffek, on pages 78–79.

Tandem Start-up

The solo start-up stroke combination should by now be a familiar method for getting up speed in the relatively short space of an eddy. Although a tandem team has more power than a solo canoeist, they too can benefit from an improved start-up.

You learned the slice stroke on page 91 as a follow-up to the U-turn using a sliding pry. You can use the slice for the *tandem start-up* in the following way: If the bow paddler's stroke is of the same strength or weaker than the stern paddler's, then the bow paddler uses a slice stroke instead of a forward stroke. This corrects the tendency of the bow to turn toward the onside. It means that the stern paddler only need take a forward stroke. Remember, correction strokes slow the canoe down. If, however, the bow paddler is much stronger than the stern paddler, then their forward strokes will balance each other out and no slice strokes are necessary.

Work out the best fast-forward combination with your tandem partner and then use it consistently every time you have to start up from a dead stop.

Tandem Offside Peel-out

1 Figure out the best tandem start-up stroke combination to get you to maximum speed when crossing the eddy line. The stroke combination performed here is a slice stroke in the bow and a forward stroke in the stern, followed up with forward strokes in both bow and stern.

2 Establish your speed, edge, and angle before crossing the eddy line. The bow paddler uses a forward quarter sweep in the entering current to initiate the offside peel-out (or in flatwater terms, the offside U-turn).

3 The bow paddler plants a cross Duffek in the entering current. The stern paddler does a reverse sweeping low brace. The canoe is now on the offside circle, an easier arc for the tandem team since the stern controls edging.

To review this maneuver on flatwater, see the Tandem Offside U-Turn Using a Cross Duffek on pages 90–91.

4 *The canoe is edging prominently into the offside turn. Both paddlers keep their bodies in the correct J-lean position. The bow paddler holds the cross Duffek as an anchor, bringing the bow to the paddle.*

5 *Both paddlers follow up with forward strokes. Looking ahead, decide on where you are going. Start setting the correct edge and angle for the next eddy turn.*

Solo Offside C-Turns

Once you are familiar with paddling inside circles to the onside and offside, having practiced eddy turns and peel-outs, it is time to put them together to perform *C-turns*. This is one of the three kinds of C-turns. This C-turn is used to peel out of one eddy and enter the next eddy downstream on the same side of the river. If you draw a line following the path of the canoe during a C-turn, it carves the letter C, or an inverted C.

1 *Employing the solo start-up for the offside circle, the paddler attains the necessary forward momentum using only three strokes to cross the eddy line.*

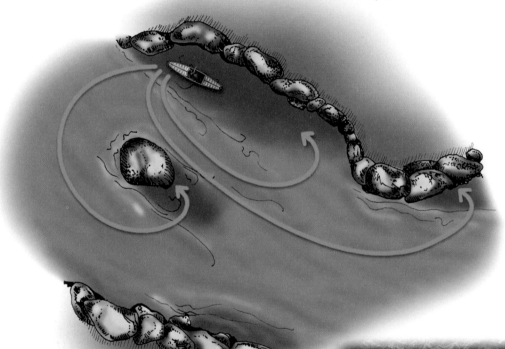

To review this maneuver on flatwater, see the Solo Offside U-Turn Using a Cross Duffek, on pages 82–83.

2   *The bow crosses the eddy line at the top of the eddy on an angle of 45 degrees or greater. Edge into the turn.*

3   *You are on the offside circle and therefore you need only to use cross forward strokes.*

4   *The paddler takes only three cross forwards to arrive at the top of the next eddy. The canoe is already angled at greater than 45 degrees to the entering current. Continue paddling the inside circle, edging into the turn and maintaining speed.*

5   *The canoe crosses the eddy line at the top of the eddy with speed, edging into the turn. Plant a cross Duffek in the entering current, the eddy. You have not taken an onside stroke since leaving the previous eddy.*

6   *The cross Duffek planted in the entering current is the stationary point around which the canoe turns. Notice the all-important rotation of the paddler's upper body, keeping it within the paddler's box.*

7   *By maintaining the offside circle while performing a C-turn, you need only concern yourself with the canoe's angle while peeling out and again when making the eddy turn. Think ahead. Before you peel out, you should already be planning the next eddy turn.*

Tandem Offside C-Turn

1 The plan is to peel out and enter the next eddy downstream on river right. The tandem canoe has lots of momentum as the bow is driven into the entering current on an angle greater than 45 degrees.

2 The bow paddler executes a cross Duffek, and the stern paddler, a reverse sweeping low brace. The bow paddler follows through from the cross Duffek with cross forward strokes.

3 You are on an offside circle, which, for a tandem team, is easy to hold because the stern paddler holds the edge.

4 The stern paddler continues with forward strokes and ensures proper canoe angle before crossing the eddy line. The bow paddler anchors the cross Duffek in the entering current (the eddy) and the stern paddler assists with a reverse sweeping low brace.

5 The bow paddler holds the cross Duffek until the bow meets the blade, and then makes a smooth transition into a cross forward. The stern paddler turns the reverse sweeping low brace into a forward stroke.

6 The bow paddler follows through with a forward stroke in unison with the stern paddler's stroke. Paddle up the eddy and peel out for the next maneuver.

When the canoe rises clear off the back of a wave taking me, the bow paddler, with it, I am a breaching whale surging up through the ocean's surface.

The Magic of Ferries

When paddlers speak of *ferries,* the uninitiated might imagine tiny canoes flitting around on stardust wings. With practice, you will eventually feel that way as you zip magically across the current, gliding effortlessly from one riverbank to another, from eddy to eddy. Ferries are one of the most common maneuvers performed on the river.

When you are ferrying, the same end of the canoe remains upstream from shore to shore or eddy to eddy. In the case of *forward ferries* (also called upstream ferries), this means the bow of the canoe faces upstream at all times. In the case of *back ferries* (downstream ferries), the bow faces downstream at all times.

In order for ferries to work, the canoe has to be set at an angle to the current. The current is deflected off the leading end of the canoe, creating a lateral force that assists with the canoe's movement across the river. (Too little angle between the canoe and the current means that you are paddling straight upstream against the river's force. Too much angle means you are turning broadside to the current and the canoe is getting pushed downstream.)

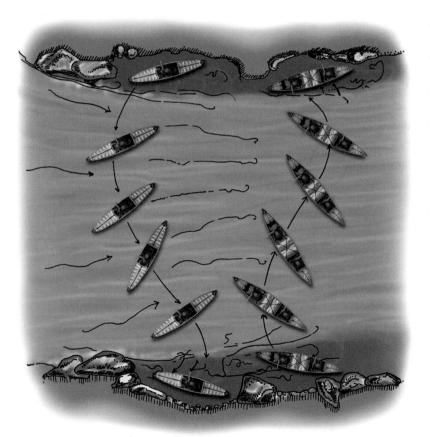

The easiest place to learn how to ferry is on swift water without obstacles or in a simple wave train that ends in a deep pool. Ideally there are two clearly defined eddies on either side of the river that you can ferry back and forth between. It is also easiest to start with forward ferries, where your bow is facing upstream.

The trickiest part of ferrying is leaving the eddy. Have a good look at the direction of the current flowing past the obstacle that creates the eddies in the photos of ferries on pages 160–164. The current direction is not uniform all the way across the river, therefore your ferry angle will need to change as you move across the river. Instead of the traditional hard-work approach to ferrying, which requires that you maintain a fixed angle in your ferry from the beginning to the end, the approach here is once again composed of smoothly linked arcs. An efficient forward ferry employs the inside circle, which means correction strokes are not necessary. Forward strokes are used throughout.

Before you do anything, concentrate on where you are going. Look at your destination eddy, *not* the eddy you are in, and *not* the eddy line you are about to cross or the entering current you are about to hit. Look at where you are going. As in throwing a ball or a dart, smooth follow-through is only possible if you are concentrating on the end result.

You need speed as you cross the eddy line. This is where the solo start-up comes into play once again. Cross the eddy line at the top of the eddy where the line is most defined. Leave the eddy with a shallow angle to the entering current, keeping the canoe aimed nearly upstream. (It is easy to get the leading end of the canoe swept downstream if your angle is too wide.)

Once you are out in the current, continue on your shallow arc path, gradually increasing the angle of the canoe to the current. You do this by making slight adjustments in your forward control stroke and in edging the canoe.

When a tandem canoe performs a forward ferry across the current, the same idea of the shallow arc applies. Establish momentum before leaving the eddy, edge the canoe slightly in the direction you are going, and paddle the arc. Both paddlers can provide momentum but it is easier for the stern paddler to adjust the edge and angle to keep the canoe on the arc.

More than anything else, keep in mind that you are attempting to incorporate the inside circle concept into your ferries just as you have with eddy turns, peel-outs, and C-turns. Paddle a sweeping, shallow S toward your destination eddy rather than maintaining a fixed angle, and you will all of a sudden feel as if you are the fairy flitting effortlessly across the current.

A Note about Resistances

In all ferries, the canoe's descent is slowed or halted. Since the canoe is traveling slower than the current, the greater force against the canoe is on the canoe's upstream (frontal-resistance) end. The downstream end of the canoe has the least resistance. It is the eddy-resistance end. If you remember the discussion of resistances in Chapter 4, you'll recall that propulsion strokes are most effective in the frontal-resistance end, and corrective strokes, in the eddy-resistance end. This means that the upstream paddler maintains the canoe's position in the river while the downstream paddler adjusts the angle if it is needed.

Descending the rapids through a rock cut before entering the challenging Thirty Dollar Rapids on the Magnetawan River.

Solo Forward Ferry

1   *Use the solo start-up to get up enough speed before you leave the eddy. You are already beginning to carve the graceful arc that will carry you across the river.*

2   *In order to ferry, leave the eddy with a shallow angle. If you accidently lose the angle, peel out, edging in the direction of the turn, and recover with a C-turn.*

3   *Paddle a shallow arc on the inside circle, in this example an offside circle, to the point of transition between the two arcs. The paddler is switching from his offside to his onside circle.*

Tandem Forward Ferry

1   *Position your canoe in the eddy beside the wave you want to ferry across. Approach as in a solo ferry. You are paddling forward on an inside circle. The stern paddler controls the angle with a stern pry or stern draw.*

2   *Edge the canoe in the direction you want to go. The stern paddler sets the angle for crossing the eddy line. Aim to leave the eddy with a shallow angle so that you don't do an unintended peel-out.*

3   *The idea is to carve a shallow arc, paddling a partial inside circle, varying the canoe's angle in relation to the direction of the current.*

4 Maintaining forward momentum throughout the ferry is easy if you are paddling arcs. Look toward your destination eddy and let the current work for you.

5 Aim to use only forward and forward control strokes, which provide power, instead of corrective strokes, which slow you down.

6 By carving two shallow arcs, thus varying the canoe's angle, you are much better able to take advantage of the current to move you laterally.

4 Using the current's lateral force to full advantage takes practice. The smooth arc you want comes from a combination of edging and angle that you adjust as you ferry across the river.

5 To enter the eddy, complete the shallow sweeping S by edging the canoe upstream onto your other circle. The bow paddler plants a cross Duffek in the eddy and the stern paddler uses the reverse sweeping low brace.

6 Eddies offer a good place for a tandem team to discuss the approach to the next part of a river run.

Tandem Back Ferry

In a *back ferry* the canoeists are facing downstream and back paddling to slow the canoe's descent. With this technique you can take advantage of the ferry action to move laterally across the river while still looking downstream. There are two things to keep in mind while making a back ferry. Forward paddling is more familiar than back paddling, so it is natural to find any maneuver done backward more challenging. Second, back ferries are more often initiated while in the current rather than from an eddy. In the current you have a lot of downstream speed (as opposed to a forward ferry, which starts in an eddy with upstream momentum). This means you have to really put the brakes on with strong back strokes and establish an acute angle to the current in order for the back ferry to be effective. You may find the back ferry confusing because you have to actually aim the bow of the canoe in the direction you are trying to avoid. Your stern is instead pointing in the direction you want to go.

Back ferries are especially useful for a heavily loaded tandem canoe, which may not have the time or the space in which to spin into a forward ferry position before the canoe is upon an obstacle. This "obstacle" would be not so much a single rock or boulder that could be avoided with a simple sideslip, but rather a ledge that required the canoe to move laterally for a distance. By being able to keep the bow facing downstream, you can back ferry above a ledge, while at the same time easily seeking the best way down. Once you have back ferried the canoe to a safe channel, simply straighten the canoe out so it is parallel with the current and then carry on downstream.

The back ferry is also useful in the case of catching an eddy on the inside of a riverbend. Let's say the river is narrow and there's a big tree overhanging the outside of the riverbend. You will want to use the back ferry to end up in the eddy downstream of the inside curve. This is also called a *riverbend set*. You set up a sharp ferry angle so that the stern (now the upstream end) points toward the river's inside curve.

In the photos on page 164, the canoe is approaching a ledge on river right. In order to scout the route, we back paddle to slow the downstream movement of the canoe and back ferry toward river left where there is a clear channel. The back ferry enables us to maintain a downstream discipline so we can both easily see the ledge and determine a suitable passage around it.

The roles of the two paddlers are reversed as soon as you paddle backward. The difficulty for the bow paddler, who now has the responsibility of setting the canoe's angle, is that he cannot see the canoe's angle in relation to the current. When the canoe is going forward, the stern paddler can see the entire canoe in front of him. When the canoe is going backward, the bow paddler catches only glimpses of the scene over his shoulder. Back ferrying is a highly useful skill, especially for tandem canoeing on river trips. It is a cautious and wise approach when you are scouting your route from a heavily loaded canoe.

1 *Whether you are going forward or backward, speed, edge, and angle are needed before you leave the eddy. For a solo paddler, the compound back stroke works well. A tandem team uses back strokes.*

4 *In this sequence, we left the eddy paddling an onside circle. Partway across, we level the canoe and then edge the canoe into the offside circle. This puts the canoe on the correct arc and angle to catch the eddy.*

2 The bow paddler, now in the eddy-resistance end of the canoe, establishes the edge and holds the canoe on a shallow angle so that it does not peel out. The stern paddler's main function is to provide propulsion. Remember the shallow S-turn of the forward ferry? It applies to the back ferry too.

3 Here you can see the canoe is already carving a shallow arc, edging to the inside of the circle. As with forward ferrying, paddling the arc of a shallow S rather than maintaining a fixed angle should be your goal.

5 Cross the eddy line, maintaining your speed, edge, and angle.

6 The ferry is complete when the destination eddy has been reached. Keep edging to the offside as long as you still have momentum. (If you level the canoe out quickly, you'll drop the side of opposition, risking a capsize.)

Tandem Back Ferry to Avoid an Obstacle

1 The back ferry is a very useful technique for moving laterally across the river to scout the route or avoid a river obstacle. Both paddlers use back strokes.

2 The bow paddler increases the ferry angle using reverse quarter sweeps. The stern paddler provides momentum. Point the stern in the direction in which you wish to move.

3 Here, we have angled our stern toward river left. You need a considerable angle and strong back strokes to make it work.

4 We are working our way past the ledge to a safe channel on river left.

5 The slower current in the mid-river white eddy assists us in our back ferry to river left. Upon reaching the desired channel, the bow paddler uses a quarter forward sweep to straighten out the canoe.

6 Back ferrying enables you to watch where you are going throughout the entire crossing. Once the ferry is complete, simply return to forward strokes.

While mapping out the route for the Ancient Forest Water Trail, we portaged and canoed 1,200 miles (1,900 km) across Northern Ontario, traveling upstream and downstream on more than a dozen different rivers including this, the Spanish River, with its beautiful valleys and pine forests.

Solo S-Turn, River Right to River Left

S-turns, like C-turns, get you from one eddy to another. However, in performing a C-turn you stay on the same inside circle throughout. For S-turns you have to change from one inside circle to another. Refer back to Chapter 17, Paddling in Circles and Arcs, to review your figure eights. An S-turn is the better part of a figure eight. S-turns enable you to catch all the eddies you couldn't catch doing a C-turn. While ferrying, you were learning the art of using shallow S-turns instead of fixed angles.

The S-turn is a combination of a peel-out and an eddy turn. Another way of envisioning this is to think of it as paddling your onside circle and your offside circle. Use the solo start-up to initiate the first half of the S-turn.

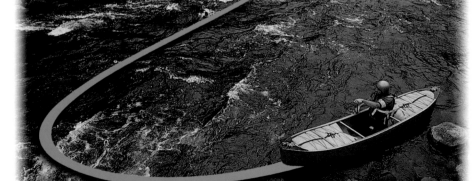

1   *Peel out at the top of the eddy with speed, edge, and angle. You are in control, paddling the onside circle.*

2   *Paddle the arc of the inside circle and you won't need corrective strokes. You are putting all your effort into forward propulsion.*

3   *Maintain your forward speed across the current with forward and forward control strokes.*

4   *Initiate the change in circles from the onside to the offside by taking a forward sweep. At the same time, edge to the offside. This is the S-turn and it prepares you for entering the eddy.*

5   *Plant a cross Duffek in the entering current (the eddy). The canoe turns around this anchor point. Continue edging the canoe in the direction of the turn.*

6   *Once the bow meets the blade on the cross Duffek, take a smooth cross forward stroke. No momentum is lost. You are ready to peel out again.*

Solo S-Turn, River Left to River Right

1 *Use the solo start-up to initiate the offside circle before you leave the eddy.*

2 *Edge into the turn. (Remember your J-lean.) Plant the cross Duffek in the entering current (the main current). Think of the peel-out as a flatwater U-turn. Pretend there is a marker buoy at the top of the eddy.*

3 *Focus on and paddle toward the top of your destination eddy. Complete the second half of the S by going from one inside circle to the other. In this demonstration, the paddler is going from an offside circle to an onside circle.*

4 *You are now edging into the turn, using an onside circle with the canoe correctly oriented to the eddy line. Keep paddling forward to maintain speed to cross the eddy line.*

5 *When you plant the Duffek in the entering current, the canoe continues edging into the turn, with the bow being drawn toward the blade. Remember to keep your upper body within the paddler's box.*

6 *To catch a small eddy, execute more of the turn in the leaving current.*

Spring is the ideal time to run the Dog River from its headwaters to Lake Superior. The whitewater is at its best, the wildflowers are blooming, and the song of the winter wren echoes in the dark gorges.

7 Notice the force of the water against the stern on the outside of the turn. Because the stern is still moving laterally against the water, it is important to continue edging in the direction of the turn. (In other words, keep the side of opposition raised until the canoe stops.)

Tandem S-Turn, River Left to River Right

The tandem S-turn is a maneuver that combines paddling your onside and offside circles in partial figure eights. Once you start thinking about the path you want your canoe to make, the appropriate strokes will come naturally. Perform them in unison and your paddling will be smooth and appear effortless.

1 *Establish momentum and begin carving the inside circle before leaving the eddy. In this case, we are peeling out on our onside circle.*

2 Cross the eddy line, edging the canoe in the direction of the turn. The bow paddler plants a Duffek, and the stern paddler uses stern sweeps to bring the stern around.

3 Maintain your forward speed and direction using forward strokes. Keep your eye on the top of your destination eddy.

4 The bow paddler uses a forward quarter sweep to assist in changing arcs in the middle of the S-turn. This is the transition point on the figure eight. Both paddlers edge to the inside of the new circle, the offside circle.

5 Edge into this offside arc with speed and a 45-degree or greater angle to cross the eddy line. The bow paddler plants the cross Duffek in the entering current (the eddy). Notice the upper bodies of both paddlers are within the paddler's box and are J-leaning.

6 Maintain edging throughout the turn. The bow paddler holds the cross Duffek, allowing the bow to meet the planted blade. The stern paddler uses a reverse sweeping low brace.

7 Following the cross Duffek, the bow paddler takes a cross forward then a forward stroke. The stern paddler follows the reverse sweeping low brace with a forward and another forward stroke. Paddling in sync as a team adds greatly to your efficiency and grace on the water.

1. We are preparing to do a peel-out for an S-turn. The stern paddler establishes the angle while the bow paddler provides the forward momentum.

2. Cross the eddy line at the top of the eddy. Establish the inside circle (here, an offside circle) with both paddlers edging to the inside of the turn. The bow paddler plants a cross Duffek to bring the bow around.

3. Paddle across the current with forward strokes. This is the transition stage between the two arcs, where the canoe is level.

4. By paddling on the inside circle, both paddlers are using forward strokes, maintaining strong momentum. By paddling faster than the current, you can control your course.

5. Upon reaching the destination eddy, the bow paddler plants a Duffek in the entering current, around which the canoe turns. The stern paddler uses stern sweeps to bring the stern around faster. Keep edging to the onside.

6. To become a smooth tandem team, practice paddling sections of river without stopping. Paddle continuously linking arcs, drawing figure eights, and gliding through smooth S-turns and C-turns.

Negotiating a narrow chute on Temagami's Matabitchuan River brings back fond memories of our first whitewater trip together, when Gary introduced me to a favorite northern river he grew up with, paddling on it since childhood.

The throw bag, a stuff sack full of flotable polypropylene rope, is the primary rescue tool used by paddlers on the river. With practice it can be deployed quickly and accurately. Yell "Rope," or whistle to make eye contact with the swimmer. Then yell "Rope" a second time as you actually throw the bag.

19 Río River Rescues and Safety

The keys to canoeing safety and accident prevention are a respect and knowledge for the power of moving water and the potential hazards created by it, developing good canoeing skills in whitewater, understanding the capabilities of your equipment, and ensuring that there is reliable communication between the paddlers in your group. A full repertoire of rescue procedures comes with experience, and developing these should be as much a part of river running as working on smooth eddy turns and peel-outs. Practice scenarios in controlled conditions. Your training will help you face a wide range of situations with calm, competent responses. The more stressful the circumstances, the more valuable this kind of reaction will be. Anticipate potential difficulties. Ask the questions "What if this happens? What are my options? How can I respond? Am I willing to assume responsibility for my actions?"

River safety and river rescue technique is, like first aid, best learned under expert instruction where you can participate in a variety of real-life scenarios. In this chapter, we cover only the basic skills of self-rescue, canoe-assisted rescues, and shore-based rescues.

Rescues start with a simple set of priorities. People first, then canoes, then equipment. Rescues always begin with the premise that you are responsible for helping yourself. Never depend on others to come to your aid.

Self Rescues

Assuming a self-rescue attitude is your most important first step after tipping over. If you are going to be playing around in whitewater, paddling fully outfitted whitewater canoes (as shown), the easiest and safest method of self-rescue, under most circumstances, is to *stay in the canoe* and right it again with a roll. Learning the open canoe roll is the responsible and smart thing to do. Not only does it help you and your paddling companions, it also increases your confidence.

You will learn faster and easier if you don't have to keep worrying about an unpleasant swim. Kayaks have probably been rolled from the time people first constructed and paddled them in Arctic waters thousands of years ago. Rolling an open canoe, in comparison, is a modern-day invention, made possible by whitewater outfitting systems.

Capsizes are a part of whitewater paddling. The occasional unintended swim happens to the best of the best. Common causes for capsizing the canoe are failure to edge the canoe in the direction it is turning, broaching on river obstacles, and swamping in large waves or swirly currents and eddy boils. You should practice the technique for swimming safely in rapids with and without your equipment so that when it happens you can respond without having to think.

The Open Canoe Roll

The four steps to the *open canoe roll* include the learning setup, the sweep to right angles, the conversion to a low brace, and the roll itself.

The learning setup is important while you are trying to master the roll. Once in position (as described in Photo 1), picture yourself upside down. Everything in the air will be in the water, everything usually in the water will be in the air. Once you have a reliable roll, you will want to develop the *slice setup,* which is faster. Instead of setting up as shown, just tip to your offside and slice the blade under the canoe, bringing it to the surface at right angles. You are immediately ready to make the conversion to a low brace.

Because the open canoe is a bulkier craft, it is rolled more slowly than a kayak. In fact, if you rush the roll, it will be harder to do. Keep your upper body relaxed and roll the canoe up with your lower body. Before you tip, make sure your thigh straps and foot braces are properly adjusted for a safe and comfortable fit.

The Wet Exit

If you tip a canoe that is not outfitted with thigh straps and toe blocks, you will just fall out of the canoe. Immediately assume the *safe swimmer position* as described on page 180. If you are in an outfitted canoe and you fail to roll, either because you can't or you try and fail, then you must make a wet exit from the canoe. Upon capsize, *wet exit* the canoe. Practice your wet exit on flatwater and in deep moving water until your natural reaction is to take these actions: Tuck your body forward to protect your head and face as well as make the exit easier. When you take your feet off the foot pegs, the thigh straps will slip off your thighs, allowing you to simply fall out of the canoe. If you are paddling tandem, make sure your partner is also out of the canoe and okay. Confirm this by voice: "Are you okay?" *Get to the upstream side of the canoe, hold on to your paddle and grab the painter on the end of the canoe nearest the safest shore.* (Review Chapter 15, Preparing for the River, on safely outfitting a whitewater canoe.)

The Solo Roll

1 The learning setup: Cross your paddle to your offside. Hold it flat over the water beside the canoe with the powerface up. The shaft is parallel to the canoe's centerline. The knuckles of your shaft hand are down. Push both hands and the paddle underwater.

5 The conversion to a low brace: Flip the blade into the low brace position, control thumb forward and powerface up. Roll your body on top of the paddle shaft. Look down. Your control hand is at your belly button and your shaft hand is at your forehead.

2 *Tuck your upper body and head as far forward as possible. Edge to your offside until the gunwale goes underwater. Keep lifting with your onside knee until you have rolled 180 degrees, meaning you are upside down.*

3 *The sweep to right angles: Break the surface with your hands and the paddle. The blade is on a climbing angle with the powerface down against the surface.*

4 *Sweep the blade and your body until both are at right angles to the canoe's centerline. Your head is tucked against your offside shoulder (here, the left shoulder). At this point, the paddle blade's powerface is turned down against the surface.*

6 *Your arms, shoulders, and neck should be relaxed as you exert force on the canoe with your legs. Press your offside knee into the hull and lift with your onside knee.*

7 *The roll: Sweep your upper body and the paddle forward, keeping the blade on a climbing angle. Keep your head down until your body passes the centerline.*

8 *For a successful roll, remember to first keep your head down until the canoe has righted; second, push and pull with your legs and abdominal muscles, keeping your upper body relaxed; and third, don't press down on the blade.*

The Tandem Roll

The *tandem roll* is a more advanced move simply because it takes the coordination of two people trying to do something upside down and backward. We think it's just plain fun to attempt such moves and very satisfying when you do sucessfully roll tandem in a river situation. Learning to roll tandem is like any other tandem move. You have by far the greatest success when you have learned to do it solo first.

Get out your scuba masks and practice this on flatwater on a day when the water's warm. The fun thing is not only that you can see what you are doing, but you can get a breath between tries by tucking your head forward into the air space of the upside-down canoe. You can even hold a conversation with your partner, much to the amusement of people on the surface nearby.

After the canoe has flipped, either the stern or bow paddler has to switch sides since you have to have both paddles on the same side of the canoe to roll it. We find it is easiest for the bow paddler to change sides. The synchronization of the roll is accomplished more by feel than anything else. When the stern paddler feels the bow paddler initiating the roll with the sweep to right angles, he immediately does the same. It's most important to get the timing together when you are using your legs and abdominal muscles to right the canoe.

*Whether on a surfing wave or
on a river journey to the sea, think of
dancing your canoe to the rhythm of the river.*

1 The learning setup: A tandem roll begins with two paddlers who already have strong solo rolls. You have to decide who is going to change paddling sides and then stick with it.

2 Once you have tipped over, give the bow paddler a few seconds to switch paddling sides and get oriented. The object is to synchronize your rolls as closely as possible.

3 The sweep to right angles: Set the blades at a slight climbing angle at the surface. Sweep your paddles to right angles with the centerline. Follow the sweep of your blade with your upper body.

4 The conversion to a low brace and the roll: Turn your control thumb forward. The powerface is flipped up. Look down. Relax your upper body and arms. Roll the canoe back up with your legs by pushing down with your offside knee and lifting your onside knee. Tighten your abdominal muscles as you sweep your blade forward.

5 Don't push down on the blade and don't lift your upper body. Think of rolling the canoe up the way a roller blind rolls up the window covering. The material hangs loose and is rolled back onto the roll. The paddler and paddle are at the free end, getting rolled back up by the push and pull of legs and abdominal muscles, not the muscles of the upper body.

6 Sit up only when your nose and upper body have crossed the centerline. Once upright, the canoe is fairly hefty with all that water sloshing around. Be ready with your righting strokes to prevent another capsize.

The Safe Swimmer Position

Upon capsizing or wet exiting the canoe, assume the *safe swimmer position*. That means you are *on your back with your feet out front at the surface* to deflect any downstream obstacle. That way you also avoid getting your feet trapped in anything beneath the surface. Use one hand to hold your paddle and, if possible, the canoe's painter, and the other arm to swim aggressively to the safest shore.

The *safest shore* may be the inside riverbend where the water is slower and shallower, a beach or gravel bar instead of a rock cliff, or it may be best to follow the safe deep channel through a rock garden, waiting until you reach the pool at the end of the rapids. If you are swimming to river right, use your right arm to swim with; if swimming to river left, use your left arm. Use a sidestroke or lifeguard stroke so you can watch where you are going while swimming and holding your equipment. Hold your canoe by the painter so you can let it drift down and away from you. You can direct the canoe's path by swinging it below you.

There are *exceptions to the feet-first swimming position*. If it looks as if you are headed for a strainer, immediately turn over and swim toward it so you can climb up onto the branches rather than be pulled down under them. If you find yourself about to drop over a ledge, tuck into a ball. This helps protect your limbs, especially your feet, from entrapment in rock crevices below the drop.

Tandem Self-Rescue

1 *Your priority is to get yourself safely to shore, but a well-practiced self-rescue procedure often means you can get your equipment safely to shore as well, instead of strewn down the river. Upon capsize, wet exit.*

2 *Call to make sure your partner is okay and get upstream of the canoe. Remember the tremendous weight of moving water; under no circumstances should you risk getting pinned between your canoe and a rock. Hang on to your paddle.*

3 *Either the swimmer closest to shore or the strongest swimmer can grab the canoe painter. Let the canoe swing downstream away from you and begin swimming aggressively to shore. Try to keep control of the canoe by swinging it past obstacles.*

4 *Swim to the nearest safe shore.*

Reentry from Deep Water

If you capsize some distance from shore, and the river flows into a big, deep pool, it is possible to make a deep-water reentry. This depends on your agility and it is much easier to do tandem than solo. A canoe outfitted with airbags displaces a lot of water, so when it is flipped upright, it rides fairly high on the surface. Two paddlers get on either side of the canoe. Using a scissor kick, both paddlers hoist themselves up and into the canoe. Keep your weight over the centerline. Reach across to the opposite gunwale, twist, and flop into the canoe.

1 If you end up in a deep pool a distance from shore, you can use a deep-water reentry. This is easier with a tandem team than in a solo canoe because the two paddlers counterbalance one another. Hold on to your paddles and roll the canoe right-side up.

2 Place your paddles inside the canoe. The airbags displace enough water that the canoe is not swamped and retains a fair bit of freeboard.

3 With the two paddlers at either end of the canoe and on either side of it, count to three and then hoist yourselves up onto the gunwales. With paddlers of uneven weight it is easier if the heavier paddler swings his weight over the centerline first.

4 Paddle to shore and empty the canoe.

Canoe-Assisted Rescues

1 The canoeist in the eddy goes to the assistance of the paddler who has just capsized. Peel out and approach the swimmer, staying upstream of the capsized canoe.

2 Assisting a fellow paddler begins with the work of the rescuee (the swimmer). This person assumes the self-rescue tactics of getting upstream of the capsized canoe, hanging on to his paddle and canoe, and swimming vigorously to the nearest safe shore.

3 The most common canoe-assisted rescue is bumping. The rescuer approaches the swimmer and capsized canoe from upstream, placing the capsized canoe between her canoe and the nearest safe shore. Place your bow against the capsized canoe and push.

When a canoeist capsizes and a fellow paddler in a canoe comes to his aid, that is a canoe-assisted rescue. There are three common options; the first is bumping, the second is towing, and the third is canoe-over-canoe. The first two are demonstrated here. The canoe-over-canoe rescue is shown in Chapter 12, Flatwater Rescues, on pages 112–113.

The key to bumping a capsized canoe to shore is to keep that canoe in the correct ferry angle.

1 Towing is a rescue option only if it speeds up the rescuee's independent self-rescue. Spin your canoe into a front ferry position, offering your stern painter to the swimmer. Communicate with the swimmer, giving clear instruction such as "Grab my stern painter!"

2 The rescuee kicks vigorously while hanging on to his own paddle and canoe painter in one hand and the rescuer's canoe painter in the other. In this way, the rescuee is greatly assisting the rescuer, who is working hard to pull the swimmer to shore.

Emptying the Tandem Canoe

It may seem like a small thing, but having an unspoken rhythm in every aspect of your tandem partnership makes time on the river so much more enjoyable. For instance, when you are playing in the rapids, you are going to get water in the canoe. Spending less time emptying it means you spend more time on the river. By doing things with a certain method, you avoid mishaps such as capsizing in the eddy or losing a paddle when you empty the canoe.

The stern paddler gets out first while the bow paddler holds the canoe steady. Tuck your paddles into the canoe somewhere so they don't fall out when the canoe is flipped over and emptied. To get the water out that is trapped under the airbags, turn the canoe over completely and rock it back and forth. The bow paddler gets back in first while the stern paddler steadies the canoe.

Side surfing a hole is paddling in three dimensions. The thrill is in balancing amid all that power. Moving forward or backward while riding the hole comes with practice and in understanding the forces at work. It is made easier when you paddle a well-outfitted whitewater canoe.

Shore-Based Rescue with Swimmer

We always have a throw bag on hand, usually one in the canoe and one in the back pouch of our lifejackets for when we are scouting a rapid. Shore-based rescues are nearly always carried out using this invaluable piece of whitewater safety equipment. It consists of a 50- to 70-foot (15–21 m) length of flotable rope stowed in a strong, lightweight nylon bag that can be instantly deployed to assist a capsized canoeist. The rescuer holds the free end of the line with one hand and, with the other, throws the entire bag to the swimmer. The rope peels out of the bag as it flies through the air toward the swimmer.

Setting up a shore-based rescue begins with scouting the rapid from shore. While you are inspecting the rapid run from various perspectives, you have to decide if there is the likelihood of a capsize and a swimmer. If so, set up a system of rescuers in strategic locations (two or three if possible).

Rescuers should be below the site where a capsize is likely to take place, allowing for the time it takes the swimmer to surface. Select the safest shore to bring a swimmer into. Rescuers have to separate themselves based on the particular situation. The rescuer wants to make sure he has good footing, but he also wants to remember the force being exerted on the swimmer as she is swung like a pendulum into shore. Consider the path you can take along the shore to lessen the tension of the rope. The shore-based system should be in place before anyone attempts the rapid, and everyone should know the plan. An experienced paddler can run the rapid first and sit in an eddy below prepared to perform a canoe-assisted rescue if need be.

Practice your throw-bag throw on dry land. The underhand throw is the most common, though it doesn't matter as long as you practice accuracy by trying to hit a running target such as, for example, your paddling partner. The bag should be thrown beyond the swimmer, attempting to land the rope across the swimmer's arms. It is better to err on the downstream side of the swimmer with your throw. The swimmer can swim toward the rope while continuing to watch her path downstream.

1 The shore-based rescuer is in position on the nearest safe shore for rescuing a swimmer. You, the swimmer, should immediately be in self-rescue mode, swimming toward that shore.

2 The rescuer deploys the rescue rope with an accurate underhand throw aimed at you.

3 Grab the rescue line.

4   *Roll onto your back so you don't get a noseful of water when the line goes taut. Kick vigorously to assist the rescuer. You are now a heavy pendulum.*

5   *The rescuer swings you into a shoreline eddy. He moves down the shore if necessary to lessen tension on the rescue rope, making it easier for you to swim.*

6   *Stand up only when you are completely out of moving water or the water is less than knee deep. Let your rescuer and your paddling companions know you are okay by raising your arms over your head to form a big O.*

There is an art to stuffing a throw bag quickly yet ensuring that there will be no kinks in the line. Either hold the empty bag up with your pinky fingers and use your thumb and forefinger on each hand to work it into the bag, or hold the empty bag in one hand with the rope running out between your thumb and fingers. With the thumb and forefinger on your other hand, push the rope into the bag. Grab another section and push it into the bag. Foot by foot, the bag eats up the rope with no coils or loops to prevent it from deploying properly.

Should you be required to throw your rope a second time, you will have to gather it up into coils, as there is no time to restuff the bag. Split the coils, holding one section in one hand and the rest in the other. This is a little trickier to throw but can be accomplished easily with practice. It helps to scoop up some water into the bag to give it extra weight for the second throw.

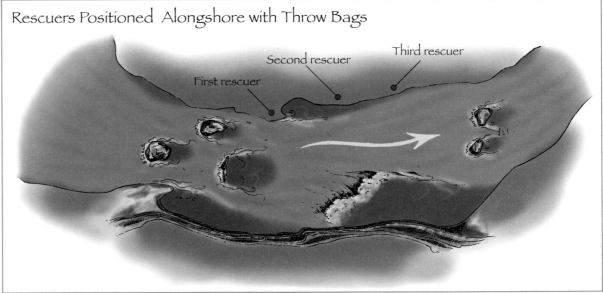

Rescuers Positioned Alongshore with Throw Bags

First rescuer

Second rescuer

Third rescuer

Shore-Based Rescue with Swimmer and Equipment

1 *Incorrect edging pitched this paddler from her canoe. Now in the water, she quickly gets to the upstream end of her upright canoe.*

2 *The swimmer grabs the canoe's painter and hangs on to her paddle. It is important to let the canoe swing downstream away from you.*

3 *The rescuer yells "Rope," or uses his whistle to attract the attention of the swimmer, who is likely disoriented. Make eye contact when you yell "Rope" for the second time. Throw the rope.*

4 *The swimmer holds her paddle and the canoe painter in one hand and uses her free arm to do a lifeguard sidestroke to the nearest safe shore.*

5 *The swimmer grabs the throw rope. The splash in the foreground of this photo is the throw bag landing across the swimmer's path. If there is more than one rescuer with a throw bag, throw only one line at a time.*

6 *The swimmer's priority is to hold on to that rope. If you have to let go of anything, it should be the canoe, not your paddle, as paddles are hard to locate later. Get up only when you can safely stand in less than knee-deep water or get out on shore.*

20 Dancing with the River

Throughout this book, we have talked a lot about paddling with efficiency and rhythm. This is particularly important in river running. Whenever you have the chance, sit by a river and watch the way it shapes the water into waves, eddies, and holes. The circle pattern is everywhere, and so we dance the river in circles, C-turns, S-turns, and figure eights.

We enjoy rapids with a variety of features, with nicely spaced eddies both mid-river and alongshore. Sometimes on a journey with a heavily laden canoe, you choose the straightforward passage down the center or the sneak route down one side to avoid large waves that fill the canoe with water. But when we are playing in whitewater as we are here, we zigzag across the current catching eddies, and ferry from one channel to another. Running rapids in this way breaks the run into a series of manageable moves. Eddy hopping means that you not only start and end a rapid in control, but that you are in control throughout. Paddling in control doesn't make running rapids any less adventuresome. It is, in fact, a whole lot more thrilling. Catching eddies and eddy hopping gives you that margin for correcting errors. It saves you the effort of continually getting out of your canoe to scout from shore, so you get ten times more fun out of every run.

One of the keys to river reading well is to look ahead at where you are going. Slalom skiers are used to doing this. For that matter, simply run along a bouldery path and see how much more successful you are when your eyes are working three steps ahead of your feet. All this takes practice, so be sure to paddle within your ability and experience.

Balancing in a headstand on the bow seat while parallel surfing is a real show of faith in your paddling partner. Besides that, it's something to do, since the stern paddler is the one doing all the work.

A great way to improve your skills is by repeating maneuvers in one part of a river, just as competitive whitewater paddlers do. Gary and I can easily spend a whole day whitewater canoeing at one set of rapids, trying every possible move to take advantage of the river features at hand. Give us a few eddies and one nice surfing wave and we are happy.

Use your intuition when running rivers. On the one hand, paddling companions can be a great encouragement. We find ourselves trying maneuvers we might not otherwise have attempted. On the other hand, the limitations of your skill may well be telling you to portage or choose another route. Remember that the difficulties of any skill are often downplayed by those who have already overcome them. Base your decision on where, how, and if you want to run a rapid when you are actually there. Conditions alter and your own circumstances change. A familiar rapid is changed by high or cold water, or if it is late in the day and you feel tired. For one reason or another, you may not always have the confidence to do something you have done before. Listen to your angel. You can always come back again another day.

Questions that should always be on your mind as you paddle rivers are "What do I do if things go wrong? What are the skills of the people I am paddling with? Do they have the ability for the river conditions? What if I capsize at the top of that rapids? Am I prepared to deal with the consequences?" If you ask these questions, you realize that you are asking them not just for yourself but for the sake of everyone. By walking around a rapid you don't feel capable of tackling, you are saving everyone the responsibility of dealing with the consequences. With river knowledge comes a kind of sixth sense that enables you to know if a hole or drop is safe, and whether you can realistically reach an eddy or ferry to a safe channel. A river-running canoeist is in a permanent state of learning by doing.

Watch the river life to learn as well. A salmon on a spawning run uses the currents to its advantage. Salmon have been perfecting the art of swimming upstream, zipping from eddy to eddy, working their way up the lesser near-shore current, for thousands of years. As canoeists, we can admire their shimmering forms and persistence, but also know what it takes to do what they do. By canoeing upstream, you can rerun rapids without portaging. Like the fish, you will dart from the top of one eddy to the bottom of another using the eddy's upstream flow to your advantage. Exit the eddies on a shallow angle and take all your strokes in the frontal-resistance end of the canoe for full power.

Canoeists who paddle rivers develop a deep respect and appreciation for water. It is no longer something you just consume or observe; it is something three-dimensional, with many personalities. You learn not to fight it. *Jet ferrying*, shown on the next two pages, is a way you can use the power of the river to your advantage in a kind of no-paddle ferry. You move with speed, with grace, with the lithe fluidity of the otter. As you jet ferry across the face of a wave, carving turns, catching eddies, peeling out, and surfing waves, then you are dancing with the river.

Solo Jet Ferry

1 Suitable waves to jet ferry are often found at the base of a steep rapid where the downstream current hits slower water.

2 Cross the eddy line with speed, edge in the direction you are ferrying, and hold a shallow upstream angle. The shallow angle is important, otherwise the fast current will grab your bow and spin it downstream.

3 Once you are jet ferrying across the wave, open up your angle to 45 degrees or more. Feel gravity pulling you into the trough of the wave. There is no need to paddle. You will be shot across the wave trough.

Tandem Jet Ferry

1 Approach with speed, edge into the turn, and establish a shallow angle as in a normal ferry. You are paddling forward on an inside circle. The stern paddler controls the angle with a stern pry or a stern draw.

2 After crossing the eddy line, open up the angle of your canoe to about 45 degrees. Feel gravity pull you in and down as you place your bow in the trough of the wave.

3 Lean back to prevent your bow from burying in the wave ahead of you. A jet ferry properly executed means that you are jetted across the current without having to take any strokes.

4 Jet ferrying, one of our favorite whitewater canoeing maneuvers, takes advantage of gravity to jet you across the upstream face of a steep wave.

5 Before entering the slower current or the eddy on the other side of this wave, be sure to edge the canoe onto your other inside circle. This change from an onside to an offside circle is particularly apparent in Photos 4 and 5.

6 Enter the eddy on your new inside circle, in this case an offside circle, using a cross Duffek followed up by cross forward strokes. Learning to see and use waves for jet ferries turns seemingly impossible current crossings into big smiles.

4 Remember that it takes two arcs to complete the ferry. Edge into the first arc, then level the canoe and edge into the second arc before crossing the eddy line.

5 The bow paddler plants a cross Duffek as the canoe edges to the offside, turning into the eddy. That was fun! When you're ready to go again, try ferrying from the other side of the wave.

Solo Parallel Surfing

The word "surfing" brings to mind a Hawaiian surfer balanced on a board, carving turns across the smooth face of a green ocean wave. On rivers there are waves to be surfed that provide equal thrills, however, your ride is altogether different. In the ocean the water stays in the same place, rising and falling as the waves pass through. On the river the water moves, rushing downhill, drawn by gravity, while the waves remain in a fixed position.

These great surfing spots can be found at the top of a hole or in a place where the river drops enough to form large standing waves. *Standing waves* form when faster flowing current meets slower moving current. Ideally, the smooth water above the standing wave or hole should be descending at an angle of 45 degrees or less so that your bow doesn't bury into the current creating the wave. It is best if the trough is at least as wide as your canoe is long. (The greater the volume of water, the wider the trough on the surfing wave.)

The trick is to first get on the wave without zipping across it in a jet ferry. This is accomplished by aligning your canoe so it is parallel with the current as soon as your bow is set in the trough. Once on the wave, the idea is to stay on it without a lot of excess paddle action. Keeping the forces balanced so your canoe remains facing upstream is a matter of placing your paddle as close to the stern as possible and making fine adjustments to the blade angle. You can adjust the angle either by setting the leading edge of your paddle blade further from the hull, which pulls the stern to the blade and turns the bow toward your offside, or by setting

1 Begin parallel surfing by leaving the eddy as if you intend to jet ferry. If you set off on your offside (shown here), hold an upstream angle by ruddering. (If you set off on your onside, use forward strokes or a stationary draw anchored close to the canoe as far aft as possible.)

2 As soon as you drop your bow into the wave's trough, align your canoe exactly parallel with the current. Set your blade as close to the hull and as far back toward the stern as possible. Adjust the angle of the blade depending on the correction you need to make. To turn the bow toward your onside (shown here), set the leading edge of the blade closer to the hull than the trailing edge.

3 To turn the bow to your offside (shown here), angle the leading edge of the blade further from the hull than the trailing edge. Lean forward to increase the weight in the bow if the wave isn't strong enough to hold your canoe. Vice versa, if gravity is pulling you down and in too far, reduce the bow weight by leaning back.

the leading edge of your paddle blade closer to the hull, which forces the stern away from the blade, causing the bow to turn toward your onside. Using the backface of the blade in this way is called *ruddering*. Ruddering is a static stroke. Remember to keep your upper body within the paddler's box. Choke up on the paddle shaft to extend the blade further back.

Once you have mastered the art of parallel surfing in one place on the wave, it's time to try carving some turns back and forth across the face of the wave. If you are starting out by jet ferrying toward your offside, as pictured here, you will switch directions to jet ferry back on your onside by using a reverse sweep.

Lean back to shift the canoe's pivot point toward the stern and edge to your onside (slightly upstream). This quick and forceful stern pivot is a *cutback*. Cutbacks occur at the outer edge of the surfing wave, enabling you to jet ferry back in the other direction without leaving the surfing wave. Hold the angle for this onside jet ferry by using either a stationary draw or forward strokes. At the outer edge of the wave, switch directions once again. This time use a forceful stern sweep while leaning back and edging the canoe to your offside (slightly upstream) to bring the bow back to the offside.

The cutback needs to happen quickly on small waves, otherwise your bow will plow into the wave ahead of you. On larger waves you can lean back and allow the downstream current to carry you up the wave face. If you lean forward, the canoe will carry you down the wave face. Once you have mastered the art of cutbacks and have the ability to control where you are on the wave face, you will swoop and glide across the river's waves as if on swallow's wings.

4 *When all the forces acting on your canoe are balanced, you are surfing the wave, magically staying in one place while the river roars by.*

After an exhilarating morning of descending the Pukaskwa's challenging rapids, nothing feels better than sitting at the water's edge on a sun-warmed rock, mesmerized by the patterns, sounds, and scents of the river.

Tandem Parallel Surfing

Tandem parallel surfing has all the thrills of surfing solo. While the current tries to force your canoe up onto the crest of the wave, gravity pulls you down into the wave trough. The thrill of riding the upstream face of a wave can be a bit intimidating the first time you attempt it. Beginning as the bow paddler with a more experienced paddler in the stern gives you confidence and a sense of the necessary balance for bringing these dynamic forces into equilibrium. There is little you can do to help the stern paddler once you are on the wave except to make slight corrections with stationary draws or stationary pries, so just enjoy the ride.

The following corrective strokes are used by the stern paddler and the solo paddler while jet ferrying and parallel surfing:

Ruddering is a static stroke that uses the backface of the blade to steer or adjust the angle of the canoe while jet ferrying to the solo paddler's offside or the tandem team's onside. Hold the paddle blade stationary and at a fixed angle in the water.

The *shallow-water pry* is a dynamic corrective stroke used to move the stern away from the blade. The stroke is performed as far aft (back) as possible. The shaft angle is low, and it helps to choke up with the shaft hand for a greater reach. Keep your upper body within the paddler's box.

The *shallow-water draw* is the dynamic corrective stroke used by the stern paddler and the solo paddler to bring the stern to the blade. Choke up on the paddle shaft and extend the paddle back with a low shaft-angle.

1 Pick your surfing wave and leave the eddy as if you are intending to jet ferry across the river.

2 Gravity draws your bow into the trough of the wave. Notice how the stern paddler is ruddering to hold the angulation. Edging and angulation are controlled by the stern paddler.

3 When the bow drops into the trough, the stern paddler aligns the stern with the bow using a shallow-water pry. Once the canoe is exactly parallel with the current, the canoe stops jet ferrying.

4 If the wave has a weak hold on your canoe, then lean forward to increase the bow's weight. If, however, gravity is pulling you into the upstream wave, back off by leaning back.

5 The stern paddler makes subtle adjustments in blade angulation to hold the canoe in its parallel surfing position.

6 The stern paddler does all the work, so the bow paddler can just enjoy the ride.

Solo Side Surfing

Solo side surfing is a rodeo ride on a bucking bronco of whitewater. A recirculating wave will easily hold your canoe perpendicular to the downstream current if the trough is longer than your canoe. The feeling of being held in the current's grasp, especially in a hole that won't let you go, makes side surfing intimidating. Start with small, gentle holes where exiting is easy. Put on your helmet and don't be afraid to wear your noseplugs, as I do. You are bound to do a few rolls!

Before going into the hole, assess two things: its shape and the angle of descent of the smooth water creating the hole. The hole should be a smiling one, meaning the corners of it face downstream so you can easily get out again. (Frowning holes mean you have to climb upstream to get out, which can be very difficult.) The smooth water dropping into the hole should be on an angle of 45 degrees or less. Any steeper and the hole becomes a keeper, and the challenge of getting into it is surpassed by the effort needed to get out again.

You can approach a hole for side surfing in two ways: from the side, as shown and described in the photos; or from above, by dropping in sideways. The latter method works best when enough water is flowing over the obstacle to allow the canoe to pass over. In this case, a white eddy forms below the obstacle, which slows the current down, preventing you from being flushed through. In this *current-broaching* method, when you turn your canoe perpendicular to the current, be sure to edge the canoe downstream *before* landing in the hole so the current doesn't catch your upstream edge and flip you.

Once in the hole, maintain a J-lean position, holding the bottom of your canoe flat on the smooth water creating the hole. It is easier to side surf a hole if your onside faces downstream. Brace with a sculling low brace or a sculling high brace if your onside faces downstream. If, however, your offside faces downstream, brace with a cross sculling high brace. To get out of the hole, put more emphasis on one side of the sculling action than on the other. This means you are either pulling yourself forward out of the hole or pushing yourself backward out of the hole while keeping constant pressure on the blade.

Side surfing is a great exercise for practicing precise boat control. Keep your upper body relatively relaxed, using only as many strokes as necessary to hold your canoe in the hole. If you can *hand roll* your canoe (rolling without the aid of a paddle), then you can toss your paddle to a friend in the eddy nearby and side surf using just your hand on the downstream side as a sculling brace.

Once you have mastered side surfing on both sides, you can attempt hole spins. These three-sixties allow you to spin in the hole so that you are facing first one way then the other without ever leaving the hole. To execute a hole spin, work one end of your canoe to one end of the hole. Let this leading end spin downstream. You may have to use forward or back strokes to prevent the entire canoe from coming out of the hole. As soon as this leading end of your canoe has swung past parallel in the downstream current (remember the other end of your canoe is being held in the hole), immediately edge to the other side while sweeping or sculling to get the canoe back into the hole facing the other way. Side surf facing in this new direction, then try spinning back the other way again.

1   *Begin in the eddy opposite the hole you want to surf. Enter it on a shallow angle, facing upstream as if you intend to parallel surf.*

2   *Entering the hole at the correct speed takes practice. If you have too much speed, you can jet ferry right through and out the other side. Go easy and let gravity pull you in.*

3   *Slide the stern end into the hole with a reverse sweeping low brace. Side surfing works well in the trough of a hole that is a little longer than your canoe. A smiling hole, where the outer edges of the hole point downstream, allows easy exiting.*

4   *Use a sculling low brace or high brace on the downstream side. J-lean your body and raise your side of opposition.*

5   *This is an example of side surfing on your onside using a sculling low brace. (You can also use a sculling high brace, where you are using the powerface instead of the backface, but keep both arms tucked into the body with your elbows down to prevent shoulder injury.)*

21 Tying It All Together

A safe and reliable roof rack and tie-down system is to your canoe what the seatbelt system is to the passengers in a vehicle. It doesn't take much to imagine the horrendous consequences of a canoe sailing off the roof of your vehicle and landing on someone's windshield. Canoes are replaceable but lives are not. The tremendous force of headwinds and the vacuum created by passing trucks should not be underestimated. The roof racks themselves need to be substantial and securely attached to the vehicle. There are various roof rack systems available that have adaptations for a wide range of vehicles and that allow you to carry all kinds of equipment. A good roof rack system will protect your vehicle roof from denting and scratches.

To tie the canoe to the roof racks, we prefer to use 1-inch (2.5 cm) webbing and cam buckles because they are fast and reliable. However some 3/8-inch (1 cm) nylon rope and a few simple knots will help you tie down boats securely on cars and canoe trailers as well.

Tie down the canoe in four places: two over the boat and two at either end. The bow and stern ropes should be attached to the vehicle's tow hooks or bumper. We have shown a tie-down system that works for us. There are many others. The key is to be sure you can trust it. We find that it is a good idea to have one person check *all* the knots. It is very easy to overlook small things such as that one small strap that didn't get tied.

Car-Topping Your Canoe

For some, the ability to easily get a canoe on and off a vehicle can mean the difference between going canoeing or not.

The *end lift* is one alternative way of lifting the canoe. (See Chapter 5, The Art of Portaging, for the side lift.) The end lift can be used by one person to get a heavy canoe into position for a one-person carry, or it can be used by one person to get the canoe onto the roof of a vehicle as shown here. (If possible, try to place the canoe deck in contact with the ground on sand or grass.)

If you are using the end lift to load the canoe onto your vehicle, lift the bow, flipping it over your head. You should end up facing forward with the stern on the ground, as in Photos 1 and 2, opposite.

1 *The end lift is a controlled way of getting your canoe onto the roof of your vehicle. Lift the bow to your knees. Place the hand nearest the bow on the opposite gunwale.*

2 *Swing the canoe up and over your head. The stern remains on the ground. You can protect the stern deck plate by placing the stern on sand or grass, or on a piece of foam or cloth.*

3 *Lower the bow to the rear roof rack. (We think it is good karma to tie the canoe onto the roof of your vehicle bow first, facing in the direction you are traveling.)*

4 *Pick up the stern and gently slide the canoe forward, keeping the bow raised until it is past the front rack.*

5 *A canoe does not rest on the roof racks at its greatest width. You may find the greatest width on a very wide canoe exceeds the width of the roof racks. When this happens, tip the canoe onto one gunwale and slide it past this point.*

6 *Lower the bow onto the front roof rack and make sure the canoe is centered and aligned. (It's scary how many canoes we see going down the highway in a ferry angle position!)*

Tying Down Canoes for Safe Transport

1   A multipurpose roof rack system, two tie-down webbing straps with cam buckles, and four end ropes are all that are needed for a reliable, time-saving way of tying your canoe down on your vehicle.

2   Loop one end of a 12-foot (3.5 m) piece of 1-inch (2.5 cm) webbing under the roof rack crossbar. Push both ends over the hull, making sure the webbing lies flat and is not twisted.

3   Thread the free end under the roof rack crossbar, back up through the buckle, and cinch it down. A rubber flap prevents the buckle from scratching the canoe. Use a couple of half hitches to secure the tail end of the webbing.

4   Get the straps across the canoe secured first and then use the butterfly knot or traveler's hitch to cinch the rope down bow and stern to the vehicle's tow hooks or bumper.

5   Make sure that you and your children, your dog, and all your gear are securely and safely attached by seatbelts or tie-down ropes inside the vehicle.

The Traveler's Hitch

1 The traveler's hitch is a quick method for tying and untying canoes on vehicles. Tie one end of the rope to the roof rack crossbar with a bowline knot. Throw the rope over the canoe. On the other side of the vehicle (and the canoe) loop the rope under that crossbar.

2 *Hold the loose end of the rope in one hand. With your free hand, grasp a bight (loop) of rope out of the rope lying across the canoe. Twist it twice, into a figure eight. Reach through the loop and grab the rope lying across the canoe. Pull this bight through to make another loop.*

3 *Feed the loose end of the rope (in your other hand) through the loop. This kind of loop works well for this purpose, but it is not a fixed loop like the butterfly.*

4 *Cinch the loose end down and tie it off with a couple of half hitches. Test the system by forcefully pushing the canoe side to side. The canoe should not budge an inch.*

5 *A simple system of ropes and knots should be easy to use, quick to adjust and undo. The straps or rope should come straight up from the roof rack on both sides of the canoe so the canoe cannot slip sideways.*

6 *To tighten ropes properly, you need a knot rigged like a pulley system. You can make a pulley system by tying any kind of loop in the line coming across the canoe. However, it is best to use a knot that can be easily undone, such as the traveler's hitch or butterfly.*

Knots

We consider rope handling and knot tying an essential part of a canoeist's repertoire of skills. Rope handling and the proper stowage of ropes are demonstrated in Chapter 15, Preparing for the River, and in Chapter 19, River Rescues and Safety. Knots are used in everything, from tying painters to the ends of your canoe to securing your canoe to the roof of your vehicle, and they are used in all manner of river rescue situations. The following knots have served us well for every eventuality we have encountered so far.

The Bowline

The bowline is a secure knot for putting a nonslip loop on a rope. To begin, make a small loop with an arm's-length free end crossing on top. Thread the free end through this small loop and under the long end, and back down through the little loop. Even under great pressure, this knot won't bind and it can later be untied.

The Sheet Bend

The sheet bend is used for tying two ropes together. It works well with ropes of different diameter as well as slippery polypropylene. Once tied, the two free ends of the ropes should be on the same side.

The Butterfly Knot

The butterfly is a simple knot, strong and secure. It will not slip once it is put in the middle of your rope. It is fairly easy to undo even after a lot of tension has been placed on it. The butterfly can be used in place of the traveler's hitch for cinching the canoe to the roof of your car.

The Fisherman's Knot

The fisherman's knot is used to tie two lines together. Make an overhand knot with each rope. We use the fisherman's knot for creating bow and stern grab-loops for all our canoes. If you use one length of rope and tie the two ends together with a fisherman's knot, you have a Prusik loop. We carry several ready-to-use Prusik loops for rescue situations.

The Figure Eight

The Prusik Knot

Take your Prusik loop and use the Prusik knot to attach it to the middle of another rope. The Prusik knot tightens under pressure and loosens when not under tension. Prusiks are very useful for whitewater rescue situations where you need an anchor point that can be moved along a rope.

The figure eight creates a secure loop. The rope can be doubled and tied as shown here. Or, to create a loop around something, make one figure eight in the rope, loop the end of the rope around the object and then trace the figure eight back with this free end.

Owain Lake, Temagami. On a journey through the forest, your passage is as fleeting as the path carved by your canoe yet, in passing, every place writes a story on your heart.

22 Paddle Your Own Canoe

The great gift of canoeing is that it can be a lifelong pursuit and highly adaptable to any individual's situation. Whether you seek the thrill of running whitewater or the tranquility of lake-to-lake paddling; whether you go alone, with children, or with friends; the humble canoe can transport you to new worlds. From a pond to a stream, from an ocean to an Arctic river, a canoe knows no bounds.

Perhaps most important, canoes can take us on a journey of changed perspective. A river paddled in the heart of a city can remind us that this urban space is built upon nature and that, no matter what we as humans do, water is central to our lives. Canoeing sets us free on the substance that not only covers three-quarters of our planet but also makes up more than seventy-five percent of our own bodies. Canoeing can make us aware of a bond that we share with all living things.

A simple paddle stroke stirs the water into a swirling vortex. We watch it spinning away as the canoe is propelled forward. The act of paddling provides a sense of freedom. The pleasure we take in it is like laughter in the way it catches us off guard. Be silent as you paddle. Listen to the water and the birds, smell the plantlife and the earth, feel the air touch your skin.

When you dip your cup into the water you paddle over, "the environment" becomes suddenly something more personal. We don't just feel obliged to care; we do care. We are the environment. There is no separation.

If canoeing touches you with the same sense of kinship that has enriched our lives, then you cannot help but hold a fondness in your heart for the places the canoe takes you. You may soon find yourself dedicated to preserving the free-flowing rivers you travel on, and to safeguarding the ancient landscapes and wild places, home to a wealth of plant and animal life, that give you so much pleasure.

Canoes provide us with a means of traveling through these places, and thus sharpen our appreciation for the life within them. With a silent stroke we may drift toward a beaver lodge where two kits swim alongside their mother. On rivers, as we wend our way upstream and downstream, we feel at times like a pair of playful otters. We have had the exciting good fortune to paddle among whales and to cross paths with swimming caribou. From the seat of a canoe we have spotted grizzly bear, muskox, and so many creatures, great and small.

But canoes can take us well beyond the bounds of lakeshore, river valley, ocean coast, and island home. When we drift on a lake on a starry night, we are afloat on the mirror of our universe. We are a tiny speck, a pinprick, in a vast ocean of life. The thought leaves us in awe of our own remarkable existence and of the power of the canoe to transport us, both physically and emotionally, to destinations warmly familiar and invigoratingly foreign.

What better way to travel through life than to paddle your own canoe.

Acknowledgments

Gary and I gratefully acknowledge the following companies and individuals whose support has made this book possible.

Thanks to Jacquie Adams, Brian Drennan, Susan Elliott, Jean-Luc Lemire and Max Wickens of Nissan Canada. Both literally and figuratively, **Nissan Canada** provides us with an ongoing vehicle for our message. Our Nissan Pathfinder has been a tremendous help in getting us safely to the trailhead of our adventures, and in our efforts to promote wilderness preservation, self-propelled outdoor pursuits, and the "experiential lifestyle."

There is no better adventurer's hat than a Tilley hat! We thank Alex Tilley of **Tilley Endurables** most sincerely for his continued faith, encouragement, and support in all our endeavors, from expeditions to book writing.

Thousands of miles of rivers and lakes have passed beneath us and our Mad River canoes. Whether we are on an Arctic river, on a whitewater daytrip, or cruising along the shore of a quiet lake, there is nothing more enjoyable than paddling a really good canoe designed for a specific purpose. **Mad River Canoe** and **Voyageur** manufacture the finest quality paddlesports equipment. Thanks to Kay Henry and Rob Center for their commitment to this project, their passion for canoeing, and their company's involvement in the preservation of wild waterways.

Thanks to Jim Stohlquist of **Stohlquist WaterWare** for allowing us the ongoing use of their superb PFDs, dry apparel, drysuits, and rescue equipment for all our paddling.

We have been using **Grey Owl Paddles** on all our journeys around the world. At our request, Brian Dorfman constructed the special instructional paddles for this book. White ash and cherry served as contrasting light and dark blade faces for the flatwater paddles, and white ash and walnut for the whitewater paddles.

Tom Foster, past instructional chairperson of the American Canoe Association, provided valuable guidance and encouragement from the early stages of creating this book.

We thank Judy and Dave Harrison, past publishers of *Canoe & Kayak* magazine and originators of the North American Paddlesports Association, for their support and encouragement for all our endeavors.

As interest in paddlesports grows worldwide, the demand for good instruction and paddlesports resources continues to increase as well. For information on clubs, instructional programs, and publications, we suggest you begin with two of North America's most comprehensive paddlesports organizations. Contact **The American Canoe Association**, 7432 Alban Station Blvd., Suite B-226, Springfield, Virginia, USA 22150, and **The Canadian Recreational Canoeing Association**, Box 398, 446 Main St. W., Merrickville, Ontario, Canada KOG 1N0.

Getting all of the variables of lighting, weather, perspective, water levels, and good technique in our favor took good equipment, film, time, and luck. We would like to thank Kieran Wallace of **Stan C. Reade Photo** and **Fuji Photo**

GREY OWL PADDLES

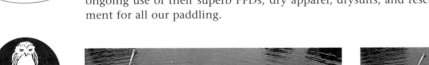

Film Canada. Most of the images were taken on Fuji Velvia, a fine-grain 50 ISO film. 100 ISO ProVia film was used in lower light situations.

Canon camera bodies and lenses are the instruments that help us capture our experiences to share with others. We would like to thank Neil Stephenson and Ian MacFarlane of **Canon Canada** for their ongoing support. Most of the instructional sequences were captured using an EOS-1N camera body and the superb AF (auto-focus) zoom lenses EF17-35mm f/2.8, EF 28-70mm f/2.8 and EF 70-200mm f/2.8.

The Macintosh 3400c laptop computer, invaluable during this book's production, was first provided to us by **Apple Canada** for a three-month canoe journey to promote protection for Northern Ontario's dwindling ancient forests. (Visit our website at **www.adventurers.org.**) We would like to thank Christine Georgiacropolus, Ralph Kamuf, Victor Chan and the staff of Apple Canada.

For years we have relied on **Lowepro** packs, camera bags and waterproof **Pelican** boxes for carrying and keeping our photographic equipment safe and dry in, on, and around the water. We would like to thank Uwe Mummenhoff, Michael Mayzel and Bud Shirley of **DayMen Outdoor Marketing** for meeting our needs as adventurers and photographers and for their personal commitment and dedication to the preservation of wilderness. **Lowe alpine** clothing and **Smartwool** socks keep us dry and warm from head to toe.

Thank you to Leslie Sparks and Janet Atkins of **Kodak Canada** for assisting us with a supply of 100 ASA Lumiere slide film the first year of acquiring instructional images. Thank you also to Dick McIntosh of Kyocera Electronics for providing the Contax RTS III and Zeiss lenses with which we began the shooting of this project.

Northern Ontario has some of the finest accessible wilderness in the world, as you can see by the photographs in this book. If you would like to explore the ancient forests, wild waterways and Lake Superior, or receive instruction in outdoor pursuits, we can highly recommend contacting Lou Pagnotta of Experience North Adventures in Sault Ste. Marie, Ontario (see www.exnorth.com).

We are grateful to our editors at **Boston Mills Press**, Kathy Fraser and Noel Hudson, for their humor, encouragement, and clarity of thought in getting us going and keeping us on track. We would also like to acknowledge Jack Stoddart and John Denison, and all those at **Stoddart Publishing** and Boston Mills Press whose various talents are important elements in the life of *Paddle Your Own Canoe*.

Creating a book, like going on a long canoe journey, is a big dream. But when it comes right down to it, big dreams only emerge from the day-to-day process. Early this morning while stretching ourselves awake in our sleeping bags, I asked my five-year-old niece Mirabai whether she was thinking about what she did yesterday or what she was going to do today. "Well, actually, Aunt Joan, I am thinking about what I am going to have for breakfast." Our family and friends both near and far (too numerous to mention by name) fill our lives with hearty breakfasts. A joke, a card, a telephone call, an impromptu invitation for supper, a sympathetic ear, a hug, a laugh, and a hundred other things are part of the magic that gets big dreams accomplished. Thank you all.

Joanie McGuffin
Goulais River, Thanksgiving 1998

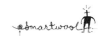

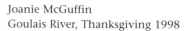

Traveling by wild waterways leads us as much inward as onward. Canoes are the remarkable vessels that make these journeys possible.